# NAVY
## FOOTBALL

# NAVY
# FOOTBALL

## RETURN TO GLORY

**T.C. CAMERON**
FOREWORD BY BILL BELICHICK

THE
History
PRESS

Published by The History Press
Charleston, SC
www.historypress.net

*Front cover*: Navy thunders onto the turf of Philadelphia's Lincoln Financial Field for the 113th Army-Navy game, a 17–13 win for the Midshipmen over the Black Knights. It was the eleventh of Navy's fourteen straight wins in the series from 2002 to 2015. *U.S. Navy/ Chad Runge.*

*Back cover inset*: The 1926 Army-Navy program celebrated the very first game ever played at Chicago's Soldier Field, a 21-all tie that set the Midshipmen up to win the program's only national championship. The game's attendance was estimated as high as 120,000, and scalpers sold tickets for as much as four times face value. *Ron Motl.*

First published 2017

Manufactured in the United States

ISBN 9781625859990

Library of Congress Control Number: 2017945023

*Notice*: The information in this book is true and complete to the best of our knowledge. It is offered without guarantee on the part of the author or The History Press. The author and The History Press disclaim all liability in connection with the use of this book.

# CONTENTS

# FOREWORD

Growing up in Annapolis, Navy football was a daily part of my family's life. My father, Steve Belichick, was an assistant coach at Navy for thirty-four years, and I was his sidekick at Navy's practices and games. I learned how to cut film and scout opponents, as well as what talents, skills and abilities to look for in a player, from him. My father taught me *how* to be a student of the game.

When I think of Navy football, my early role models were some of the biggest legends in the program's history. One of the first people I think of is Tom Lynch, a two-way player at center and linebacker. He was everything you'd want to be in a player: versatile, savvy and strong. Lynch was captain of that 1963 team, the best in Navy history, and I can't think of a better player to emulate. When I played center at Wesleyan, a lot of what I had learned was from watching Tom Lynch.

Joe Bellino and Roger Staubach were two great players—I used to catch passes for Staubach when he warmed up—but I would say that besides my father, I learned the most from watching Wayne Hardin run practices and develop game plans. He was innovative—ahead of his time in so many ways—because he understood the nuances of risk-taking. Some of the formations he could draw up, whether it be from scrimmage or within the kicking game, were brilliant.

Rick Forzano, one of Hardin's assistant coaches, is another person I learned a lot from, even though he didn't have the same level of success on the field at Navy. He went on to do a great job as head coach with the Detroit Lions under very difficult circumstances.

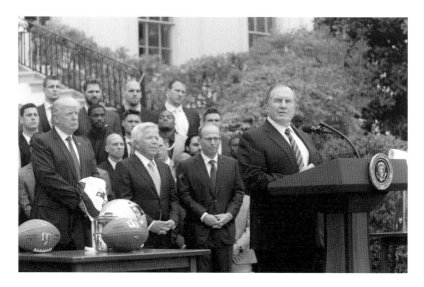

Bill Belichick speaks at White House ceremony honoring the Patriots' Super Bowl LI victory. *Official White House Photo by Shealah Craighead.*

When I reflect on Navy football, I remain impressed by how much the team means to the Navy community. Navy isn't a state-supported university; the graduates, students and staff provide the bulk of the support in and around Annapolis and the Baltimore/D.C. area.

The love for Navy football is most evident when the Mids travel nationally to play in port cities. From Jacksonville in the East to San Diego out west, you quickly see how beloved the program is by the fleet and veterans around the country.

The program had a remarkable history through the mid-1960s. Even when it fell on hard times, it continued to produce outstanding players and memorable games. Today, there's a precision to appreciate in watching the Midshipmen operate their triple-option offense; the run-pass option offenses (RPOs) dominating major college football are rooted in the principles of Navy's scheme. The discipline Navy plays with—they're hardly ever penalized—is also outstanding from a coach's perspective.

Obviously, the credit starts first with Paul Johnson, who rebuilt the program from the ground up. He handed it to Ken Niumatalolo, who has seamlessly carried on and added to the renaissance. While my affinity for the program is hardly a secret, watching the revival of Navy football during the last fifteen years has been nothing short of remarkable.

—BILL BELICHICK

# ACKNOWLEDGEMENTS

For their assistance in making this book possible, thank you to the following individuals:

Mike Peters, a fellow *Capital-Gazette* alumnus, for serving as this book's copy editor. As a writer, reporter and editor, you make a damn fine comedian. Brian Burden, also from the *Capital-Gazette*, for serving as this book's unofficial ombudsman. The *Baltimore Sun*'s Gerry Jackson, also a *Capital-Gazette* alumnus, for the local, historical perspective.

Thank you to New England Patriots' coach Bill Belichick; current Georgia Tech coach and former Navy coach Paul Johnson; current Navy head coach Ken Niumatalolo; former Navy head coaches Charlie Weatherbie, George Welsh—a former standout Midshipman player, too—and Wayne Hardin, who passed on April 12, 2017.

Thank you to former Navy assistant and current Army head coach Jeff Monken and former Air Force coach Fisher DeBerry.

Thank you to current Midshipman Myles Benning; former Midshipmen Keenan Reynolds, Alohi Gilman, Will Worth, Tom Lynch, Ram Vela, Ricky Dobbs, Eddie Meyers, Bob Riefsnyder, Evan Beard and Clint Bruce for generously sharing your unique experiences of wearing Navy's Blue and Gold.

Thank you to Naval Academy Athletic Association Director Chet Gladchuk, Vice Admiral and former Superintendent John Ryan, Deputy Athletic Director Eric Ruden, and the following Sports Information Directors or Associates: Scott Strasemeier and Stacie Michaud (Navy), Matt Faulkner (Army West Point), Troy Garnhart (Air Force) and Greg Steiner (Eastern Michigan).

Thanks to current New England Patriots' and former Navy play-by-play announcer Bob Socci, as well as current play-by-play radio man Pete Medhurst.

Thanks to Eric C. Stoykovich, historical archivist at the University of Maryland's Hornbake Library; Chris Hutson, Heisman Trust historian; Jeff Furniss and Chadwick Watson.

Final thanks to the management and staff at the Dock Street Starbucks in Annapolis; George Sparks, the "Mayor" of the Dock Street Starbucks; Cynthia Belt from the United States Naval Academy Alumni Association; John Feinstein from the *Washington Post*; Keith Meador from CollegePollArchive.com; Ohio State football writer Jim Lodico; Geoff Larcom, executive director for Media Relations at Eastern Michigan University and former sports editor of the *Ann Arbor News* (1989–99); and Jim Knight, sports information director at Central Michigan University and formerly Sunday sports editor of the *Sunday Capital-Gazette* (1986–87) and sports editor of the *Ann Arbor News* (2001–5)

I dedicate this title to two people: my late father, SGM John Scott Cameron II, and the late Ernie Harwell.

To my father, who served two tours of service in Vietnam, a tour in the 1967 Detroit riots and one tour each in Desert Shield and Desert Storm. I think of his favorite quote, "Happy to be here; proud to serve," and think, "Me too, Dad.… Me, too."

Harwell, the Hall of Fame voice of the Detroit Tigers, graciously referred me to his editors and agents ten years ago, providing me the opportunity to write books. Ernie and Paul Carey were the soundtrack of every spring, summer and fall, tucked under a pillow, atop a kitchen table or on the dock at Oak Lodge, our cottage. Everyone should be so lucky.

# INTRODUCTION

I t's never been better at Navy than it is right now.

Compare that statement to the "Camelot" days of the 1950s and 1960s, when Navy was a regular in the Associated Press' Top 20 poll, played in major bowl games like the Cotton and Sugar and battled Texas in 1963 for the national title. All of it sounds like incredible, over-the-top praise.

It is. And it's deserved, too.

Today, what strikes you from a football sense is how good the Midshipmen look physically, as good as they've ever looked in the history of the program. They're long. They're big. And when the ball snaps, they're much more athletic than they appear on film from afar. That play-making ability has been the staple of their success over the past fifteen years.

While I wrote this book, one question came up more than any other: "Why Navy?" It's fair. They're not annual contenders for the national title; the Midshipmen haven't played for the title in fifty-four years and haven't won it since 1926. They're not an over-the-top legacy brand like Alabama, Ohio State or USC. They're not Clemson, the newly appointed kings of the game after winning last year's crown and appearing back to back in the title game. And they don't wear exotic, garish uniforms like Oregon or Maryland.

What makes Navy special is they're not trying to be different—their approach to the game is as classic and time-honored as it was seventy years ago. They play some of the game's richest rivalries—Air Force, Army and Notre Dame, particularly—but service and country come first; playing on

Sunday comes second. Their offense, the triple option, is niche, an attack most fans associate with their grandfathers. But the discipline it requires, when successful, is almost like looking at artwork.

In Annapolis, a town that sails first and drinks about it later, it all works. Most of the time, the Mids fly under major college football's radar, but America's most popular spectator sport leaves plenty of room for the underdog and the upset. That's what Navy is and what Navy tries to do on most Saturday afternoons. It certainly was Navy in 2001, when they had lost twenty of twenty-one, had posted losing seasons in twenty-eight of the last thirty-eight years and were facing the humiliation of either stepping down to I-AA or facing overwhelming odds of rebuilding during major college football's never-ending arms race.

The modern-day success of the last fifteen years was unimaginable in 2000–2001, the program's darkest days. Chet Gladchuk, hired as the new athletic director on October 8, 2001, was staring at a recommendation that the program secede to the ranks of Division I-AA, but he had no intention of following orders. He fired Weatherbie with three weeks to go in 2001, tore down the structural impediments holding football and the athletic department back and simultaneously rebuilt the athletic department from the ground up.

Gladchuk was now at the wheel of a program that didn't win a home game against a Division I school from November 14, 1999, to September 20, 2003, and needed Hurricane Isabel to help break that streak. But he hired Paul Johnson, and later Ken Niumatalolo, and along with hundreds of determined Midshipmen over the last fifteen years, this trio has pulled off a remarkable comeback. The Mids defeated Eastern Michigan, 39–7, on the heels of an unimaginable hurricane that desperate September afternoon in 2003 and haven't looked back. Upsetting No. 25 and unbeaten Air Force, 28–25, in Washington, D.C., two weeks later, the Mids have reclaimed the program's past glory in the past fifteen years. That success has turned into an era of football that belongs to them exclusively.

This book connects the timeline of Navy's revival by guiding you through "Camelot," the "Long Winter" of 1964–94 and the "Big Tease" of the mid- to late 1990s. Each era is vitally important to understanding just how unlikely this "Return to Glory" was in coming to fruition.

Navy football's formative years, from 1879 to 1949, were not unlike many other schools touting rich legacies. During this era, a pair of dominant narratives emerged: the success of the Cadets and Midshipmen was part of the national morale after the country was plunged into two world wars,

Wayne Hardin is hoisted up on the shoulders of his players in front of the entire Brigade after earning the Orange Bowl bid after beating Army, 17–12. *University of Maryland/ Hornbake Library.*

and no football season was truly great in Annapolis or West Point unless it included a win in the Army-Navy game.

But the glory days of the 1950s and early 1960s—the foundation on which modern-day Navy football was built—belonged to two men: Eddie Erdelatz and Wayne Hardin. It's not at all unlike today's success. Erdelatz took the wheel in 1950 during the boom times after World War II, and it continued under Wayne Hardin, who, after Erdelatz hired him as an assistant coach in 1955, ascended to head coach in 1959. During this era, a handful of Midshipmen earned player-of-the-year awards, and Navy made regular appearances in major bowl games and national rankings. The crescendo of this era was the 1964 Cotton Bowl, when Navy played Texas for the national championship.

Navy didn't win, but those Mids, quarterbacked by Heisman Trophy winner Roger Staubach, are still regarded as the best team in school history. Unfortunately, their success created expectations that nearly toppled the program over the next forty years. From 1964 to 2002, the Mids struggled mightily, the George Welsh era from 1973 to 1981 providing the only consistent respite. Of the eight coaches Navy hired or appointed, only Welsh produced any success. Some of the players who bridged this era were outstanding, but like furniture movers, their talents were largely wasted as the program bounced from one coach to the next. Every fourth or fifth year, offensive and defensive schemes, as well as recruiting philosophies and territories, changed. Excuses piled up just as fast.

It took Air Force dominating the service academy rivalries in the 1980s and Navy's stockholders—military leaders, alumni and season ticket holders—beginning to question if Navy should continue trying to play Division I football for Navy to cry "uncle." Charlie Weatherbie, a former assistant under Fisher DeBerry at Air Force, was hired in 1995, and he went 21-13 in his first three seasons. In 1996, the Mids went 9-3 and won the Aloha Bowl on Christmas Day.

Courted by several major programs following that season, it was universally assumed that Weatherbie would leave, but he stayed. Over the next five seasons, Navy sunk back into abject failure. Instead of tip-toeing around the problems, Gladchuk doubled down, firing the coach and selling stock in a program that had produced dismal returns over most of the previous forty years. It might not have existed at first glance, but the vision of what Navy would become burned within Gladchuk, and he had the ability to sell it to those who couldn't see it for themselves.

It was a game changer at Navy. Overcoming the "Expect Two Wins" season in 2002, Johnson's vision created the fundamental changes in the football program, the Academy and the Academy's traditions to move the program into a place to succeed and then sustain that success when he left. The program has reached even greater heights under Niumatalolo, hired to succeed Johnson in 2007.

This is the inside story of how Navy said "enough" and figured out how to win, and once again win big, on college football's biggest stage.

Enjoy.

Chapter 1

# CAMELOT

## 1950–1963

**B**y the time 1950 arrived, the bloom was completely off the post–World War II rose for Navy football.

Coach Tom Hamilton had gone 2-15-1 (.138) from 1946 to 1947, and George Sauer was an equally-miserable 3-13-2 (.222) the next two years, including 0-8 in 1948.

As detailed in Jack Clary's *Navy Football: Gridiron Legends and Fighting Legends*, Sauer had been too sensitive to all the suggestions offered by senior officers at the Academy and agonized too much about what he should do with them. He agonized about pleasing his superiors so much that he pleased no one.[1]

Meanwhile, Army Coach Earl Blaik was sitting atop the crest of a wave of dominance rolling down the Hudson River. The Black Knights were national champions in 1944 and 1945, while Cadets Doc Blanchard and Glenn Davis won the Heisman Trophy in the same seasons.

West Point was dominating the rivalry and earning national prominence, too. It was time for someone who could earn the confidence of Naval Academy leadership and still have the moxie to do what he thought needed to be done to win—and win now—in Annapolis. That someone was Eddie Erdelatz.

Navy Athletic Director Howard Caldwell's only choice to fill the post, Erdelatz had been the line coach for the San Francisco 49ers in 1948 and 1949. While the Midshipmen hadn't posted a winning season since 1945—and hadn't beaten Army since 1943—Erdelatz was helping the 49ers win twenty-two of twenty-eight games.

Navy football coach Eddie Erdelatz stands with Midshipman Ned Oldham, who played at Navy from 1955 to 1957. Erdelatz went 50-28-8 from 1950 to 1959 in Annapolis. *University of Maryland/Hornbake Library.*

The lightning bolt needed to awaken a slumbering program, Erdelatz had a penchant for usurping authority. It would be the sword he fell on nine years later, but this bravado paid big dividends almost immediately. Erdelatz canceled the annual spring game, refusing to pick his starters from established letter-winners. Instead, starters, non-starters and junior varsity players would be considered for snaps based on merit in practice. Whatever previously passed for football at the Academy hadn't worked. Playing time would have to be fought for and earned.

Erdelatz knew that Navy's lack of talent and depth was severe, playing both sides of the ball had to remain the norm. The platoon system was gaining momentum nationally, but Navy wasn't good enough to abandon it. "We only played 36 guys, and you played 60 minutes for Eddie Erdelatz," said George Welsh, who played at Navy from 1953 to 1955. "There were no special teams. The punter was a player on the offense or defense, and we hardly ever had a good kicker. Making extra points was very difficult in those days because there weren't many kickers around."

Erdelatz's first season, 1950, was nothing to shout about. The year's highlight—the regular season, anyway—was a 27–14 victory over Southern California. Despite being 12-point underdogs, quarterback Bob Zastrow scored two touchdowns in Baltimore, outplaying future National Football League Hall-of-Famer Frank Gifford.

But in Philadelphia, the 2-6 Midshipmen ruined No. 2 Army's national title hopes, roaring past the undefeated Cadets in a 14–2 win. It was Army's first loss in twenty-nine games and just the third in seven seasons. This wasn't simply beating an archrival, it was a vicious takedown of one of Blaik's best teams. Like Bo Schembechler leading Michigan to a shocking 24–12 victory over No. 1 Ohio State in 1969, it took just three hours to return the pride to Annapolis.

The next year, ninety Cadets—including Blaik's son and twenty-two other football players—were separated from West Point in a cheating scandal. Over the next two seasons, Blaik scuffled to rebuild the Army program.

Meanwhile, Erdelatz was off and running, and his bravado only grew. He had served in the U.S. Navy during World War II, beginning in 1942 and rising to the rank of lieutenant commander by 1945. He also coached at Navy as an assistant, beginning in 1945, until he left for the 49ers in 1948.

Now piloting the hallowed football program in Annapolis, he took liberties, bearing a cavalier attitude to match his gregarious, outsized personality. It irritated and often alienated his military superiors. When officers made suggestions, Erdelatz was known to smile, nod and forget the offering. And in a huge no-no at a military institution, he climbed over the chain of command from time to time. When one of his players was convicted of a Class A offense, Erdelatz passed over Commandant Charles Buchanan and Superintendent Admiral C. Turner Joy to have the player reinstated. The ploy worked, but the cost was steep: Buchanan and Erdelatz never spoke again.

Three athletic directors—Ian Eddy, C. Elliott Laughlin and Slade Cutter—locked horns with Erdelatz, who wanted the football team, according to Laughlin, to "be an entity outside of the Brigade," as Clary noted in his *Gridiron Legends and Fighting Heroes*. The more superintendents, commandants and athletic directors exhorted to Erdelatz the importance of the Academy's mission and tradition, the more he chafed at the conformity required at a military institution.

Laughlin, who served as athletic director at USNA from 1954 to 1957, noted his battles with Erdelatz in an oral history recorded for the U.S.

Naval Institute, a nonprofit association that offers forums for debate on national defense issues. As detailed in Clary's *Navy Football*, Laughlin reminded Erdelatz, "You're the coach and I'm the director…so let's just work together on that basis."[2]

It worked insofar as building a winner on the field. But Laughlin, quoted in Clary's *Navy Football*, believed that Erdelatz was "a very unreasonable person who had no sense of loyalty to me, the commandant, the superintendent or the Naval Academy.…He wanted his own little kingdom and his bailiwick was the football team.…He wanted separate dorms for his team and disliked having players live in Bancroft Hall.…The football team was the only thing [of importance to Erdelatz]. But I must say, he was one heckuva football coach."

Army was decimated by the cheating scandal, but 1951 wasn't much better for the Midshipmen, although a 2-6-1 season ended with a 42–7 win over the Cadets. It was Navy's last losing season for more than a decade. Recruiting better talent, Navy made an appearance in the Associated Press Top 20 in each of the next nine seasons.

"My father wanted me to get out of the coal mines and have a job when I got out," Welsh said of being recruited by Navy. "It was just a good fit at Navy. Erdelatz was a really good defensive coach, and it was everything I could have hoped for." First recruited by Notre Dame and Penn State, Welsh was branded "too small" to be successful as a major-college player, a mistake he proved over and over at Annapolis.

Admission to the academies requires a Congressional appointment, and each state has a limit to how many appointments it can make to each academy. The "Birddog" system was a network of twenty to thirty scouts who were active around the country finding talented student athletes. Once a potential fit for the academy team was found, it was up to "Rip" Miller to find an appointment for athletes who came from an area that had already exhausted their quota for nominations.

Bob Cameron led the Mids to a 6-2-1 mark in 1952, the only losses to Notre Dame and Maryland, two of the nation's top teams. A large, stocky quarterback from California, Cameron replaced Zastrow for injury occasionally in 1951 and won the job outright the next season.

By the Army game, his shoulder was injured so badly he could barely lift it to throw or punt the ball. Still, Navy eked out a 7–0 win over the Cadets. Three wins in a row over Army and the first winning season in seven years signaled that Navy was back for good. Erdelatz was only beginning to ramp things up.

"Eddie was a 100 percent kind of guy in everything he did," said Hardin, who was hired as an assistant in 1955 and succeeded him as head coach in 1959. "He was a good man who did a great job."

## BOWL 'EM OVER

By 1954, the Mids' stock was good enough to win any game, and Erdelatz knew his team well enough to put the parts in place to make the sum successful. With Maxwell Award winner Ron Beagle at end, John Weaver and George Welsh at quarterback, Navy was primed to roll. Weaver was as shifty as Welsh, an outstanding play-caller, was sure-handed. In the split-T offense Navy employed, backs Joe Gattuso and Bob Craig averaged 7.3 and 6.4 yards per carry, respectively.

But the story of these Midshipmen was their overachievement, a spirit that showed in a 25–0 upset at favored Stanford. Navy racked up 390 yards of offense, dominating the Indians—Stanford didn't change its name to the Cardinal until 1981—despite taking on 171 yards in penalties. Stanford coach Chuck Taylor said, "I haven't seen a bunch of boys who wanted to play football more than Navy did."[3] The victory inspired a nickname: "A Team Named Desire."

George Welsh takes the snap and readies to move the ball forward for the Midshipmen. *Lucky Bag/Nimitz Library.*

Two missed PATs in a 21–19 loss at Pittsburgh and Craig's fumble before crossing the goal line in a 6–0 loss to Notre Dame in Baltimore were all that separated Navy from a perfect ledger. A thrilling 27–20 win over Army and a 21–0 whitewash of Ole Miss in the Sugar Bowl left Navy with an 8-2 record and No. 5 national ranking.

Remember the 14–2 upset of Army in 1950? Blaik did, too, and he turned the tables on Erdelatz in 1955, posting a 14–6 win. Six fumbles plus two drives that died deep in Army territory stopped the Mids, and Welsh's playing career ended unceremoniously with a 6-2-1 record.

All that stood between the Mids and the Cotton Bowl in 1956 was a win over Army, but they couldn't pull it off, settling for a 7–7 tie. Superintendent and Rear Admiral William R. Smedberg III broke the bad news in the locker room, climbing atop a foot locker and declaring, "If you're not good enough to beat Army, you're not good enough to play in the Cotton Bowl."[4]

The following year, Navy marched to eight wins, including a 21–6 win at California and a 20–6 victory over Notre Dame. Again needing to beat Army to reach the Cotton Bowl, the Mids left nothing to chance in a 14–0 shutout. Three weeks later, they whipped Rice, 20–7, for their second bowl victory in four years. Because the Academy was fundraising to build a new stadium in Annapolis, this helped enormously. With Baltimore's Colts and Orioles using Memorial Stadium on a full-time basis, the option of trekking up to Thirty-Third Street in Baltimore to play the biggest home games of the season was becoming less attractive.

Bowl games and big wins over the likes of Army, Stanford and Notre Dame helped build Navy–Marine Corps Memorial Stadium. Some at the Academy wanted the new stadium to seat as many as sixty thousand, while others worried that Annapolis wouldn't support the team if it was struggling. "Much of the support the academy generates comes from Navy people," said Belichick. "Most of the graduates aren't from Maryland, and they scatter for their service assignments when they graduate. When I see Navy play out of state in Florida, Texas, California, they draw incredibly well."

The shovels went into the stadium site on Rowe Boulevard and the calendar turned to 1958, but the sun was setting on Erdelatz. Headstrong to a fault, he had worn out his welcome over the past eight seasons. The Naval Academy Athletic Association (NAAA) was fundraising to pay the $3 million tab on the new stadium, and the last thing it needed was a coach who wasn't about the mission of "Academy first, football second."

The highlight of 1958 was a come-from-behind 20–14 win at Michigan. Late in that game, from high atop the Michigan Stadium press box, Wayne Hardin unknowingly previewed his future as head coach. Every Monday before a game, Steve Belichick went over the opponent's offense, defense and kicking team. He noted Michigan's bad habit of biting on a fake dive over the tackle into a play-action pass. "We get to the end of the game, and I said, 'We've got to throw that pass,'" Hardin said. "On the other end, they're saying, 'Michigan knows what the fake means' and I screamed, 'Get the damn play in the game!'"

"Eddie didn't hear real well on the sideline, so I said, 'I'll take all the responsibility. I know I might get fired, but we're not losing this game. Put the pass in. NOW!'" A magnificent thirty-seven-yard pass from Joe Tranchini to Dick Zembrzuski decided the issue with 5:05 remaining in the dramatic contest.[5] "Belichick had called that play in the scout meeting the Monday before the game—Boom!—It's a touchdown, and we won," Hardin said.

The Midshipmen had a respectable season at 6-3, but Army's "Lonesome End" offense, devised specifically for Pete Dawkins, was a scheme that Navy never truly figured out. The Cadets knocked off Navy, 22–6, and Dawkins became the third Cadet in fourteen years to win the Heisman Trophy.

Following the season, a tsunami of change swept over both academies. Blaik retired from West Point, and Erdelatz was moving on, too. He had secretly courted the head coaching job at Texas A&M. Erdelatz quietly visited College Station and reportedly earned the endorsement of the outgoing Paul "Bear" Bryant.

But an "Erdelatz to A&M" story found the newspapers, leaving both Navy and A&M a bit red in the face. The Aggies' administration denied the agreement, and Navy wasn't going to retain a coach looking to leave. The straw broke when Erdelatz shredded Academy leadership in public comments at an Annapolis Lions Club breakfast. He had flaunted his ability to usurp authority for nine years, had been outed trying to find another job and now was complaining he wasn't getting the support he needed? Athletic Director Slade Cutter went directly to Rear Admiral Charles L. Melson, the new superintendent, to tell him the coach must be fired immediately. "He didn't even ask why," Cutter said. "Melson said, 'It's your problem. Call a meeting of the board and see if they approve.'"[6]

Two hours later, Erdelatz was done. Whether he wanted to be fired, no one will know. But nobody walked Navy's dog like this and kept his job long enough to tell anyone about it.

## NEXT MAN UP

A full cupboard awaited Hardin, despite not being embraced as head coach by Naval Academy leadership. When the athletic board that voted to fire Erdelatz finally accepted Hardin's appointment, it wanted to cut the position's salary from the $17,000 Erdelatz was paid to $12,000. Cutter objected, saying, "By God, if you are hiring a guy to replace someone you have fired, you have to pay him as much as the guy you have just fired." The board agreed to a slight increase.[7]

The Hardin era coincided with the opening of Navy–Marine Corps Memorial Stadium, but 1959 ended with an uninspiring 5-4-1 record. During a brutal five-game stretch in the middle of the season, Navy went 0-4-1 against SMU, Syracuse, Miami, Penn and Notre Dame, a 22-all stalemate with Penn at Franklin Field the only salvation.

But in winning the last three games, Navy found a star in a 190-pound running back with tree stumps for calves: Joe Bellino. With the score tied late in an eventual 22–14 win over Maryland in Baltimore, he took a punt fifty-nine yards for a touchdown, slipping past several potential tacklers for the game-winning score. Hardin had been screaming at him to get out of bounds, thankfully to no avail. The season ended with a 43–12 trouncing of Army in Philadelphia.

In 1960, Hardin and the Mids did something that wouldn't be matched for forty-seven seasons: they beat Air Force, Notre Dame and Army in the same season. The 35–3 slaughter of Air Force in Baltimore was the first meeting between the two now-historic rivals. A 14–7 win over the Fighting Irish in Philadelphia, followed by a 17–12 win over Army when they returned four weeks later, delivered the Orange Bowl bid to the Midshipmen.

Bellino won the Heisman—Navy's first such winner after Army had three in fourteen seasons—and a 21–14 loss to Missouri did little to dampen the pride from an outstanding season and a 9-2 record. "Joe Bellino was the best one-on-one back I've ever seen," Hardin said. "We played Washington as a 40-point underdog, and we were down, 14–12. We threw a screen pass to Joe and [he] dodged every defender on the other side *twice* and made about 19 yards for a first down. Then he did it again. So now I'm torn because I don't want to give Joe the ball too much. We don't have a great kicker, so I asked Greg Mather if he could make it and he said, 'Yes.'"

Mather's kick went up and barely cleared—the *Spokesman-Review* described the ball as having "loafed" over the crossbar—and Navy won, 15–14. "The only reason we even had a chance to win was because of Bellino," Hardin said.

Joe Bellino and Joe Matalavage celebrate the trip to the 1961 Orange Bowl after defeating Army, 17–12. *University of Maryland/Hornbake Library.*

By 1963, Hardin had another dynamic player: Roger Staubach. Known as "Roger the Dodger" for his outstanding scrambling ability—or "Capt. America" and "Jolly Roger," depending on the newspaper you read—Staubach was an All-American who captured the Heisman, Navy's second in four seasons.

Navy manhandled Michigan, 26–13, in Ann Arbor, and as team captain Tom Lynch recalled, "Michigan carried seven or eight guys off the field… and Roger was like Wayne Gretzky, with that sixth sense of his. By that point, I was starting to think nothing he does would surprise me."[8]

The Mids marched into the Cotton Bowl with a 3-0 record and a No. 4 ranking but were upset, 32–28, by SMU in what the *Dallas Morning News* described as "a game that forever will be remembered as one of the most thrilling ever played at the Cotton Bowl." The game was played on a Friday night of the Texas State Fair, which hosted the more famous Oklahoma-Texas game the next day.

Clifford E. Deming presents the Heisman Trophy to Navy's Joe Bellino on December 8, 1960, in New York City. *Heisman Trophy Trust.*

Twice Navy had double-digit leads, and twice SMU roared back. Twice Staubach had to come out of the game for shoulder dislocations administered by the Mustangs' fierce front. Navy absorbed more than one hundred yards in penalties—game officials were suspended when a review revealed that they slighted Navy considerably—but the Mids still would have won if receiver Ed "Skippy" Orr hadn't dropped a touchdown pass on the final play of the game. "Staubach hit 'Skippy' right in the chest," Hardin said. "I still wake up with nightmares of [Orr] reaching out for the ball as it went off his fingertips. That's what kept us from being No. 1."

Following the heartbreak in Dallas, Navy marched to the doorstep of a national title, pounding Notre Dame (35–14), Maryland (42–7) and Duke (38–25) to set up another epic battle with Army.

The week before the game, Lee Harvey Oswald assassinated President John F. Kennedy, and in an instant, the best team in school history was

Navy's Edward "Skippy" Orr wrestles Southern Methodist tight end Johnny Graves down for a seven-yard gain in 1963. Orr dropped the potential game-winning pass in the final seconds of Navy's 32–28 loss at SMU. *University of Maryland/Hornbake Library.*

barely back-page news. The death of Kennedy crushed the team. Just a year earlier, Kennedy had shaken the hand of every player and coach on the team in Quonset Point, Rhode Island, where Navy had traveled for a training camp. Kennedy had detoured from his travels to the family compound in Hyannis Port, Massachusetts, to meet the team.

"JFK wasn't supposed to be biased, but he let us know he was a Navy [fan] and he got away with it," Alexander Krekich said. "We got to march in his inaugural parade. We had a real love for him, and we were extraordinarily sad after what happened in Dallas. We weren't sure if there would be another game to prepare for. Frankly, we didn't care."[9]

The Army-Navy game was rescued by Kennedy's widow, Jackie, who requested the game be played in her husband's honor. So, on December 7, a week later than usual, the Mids raced out to a 21–7 lead before surviving a frantic Army rally to win, 21–15. The Cadets had raced inside the Navy five-yard line in the game's last minute, but confusion reigned, and Army managed to snap the ball just once more. The clock expired with the ball on Navy's two-yard line. "The relief of not losing that game was tremendous," Staubach told Gary Lambrecht for NavySports.com. "We wouldn't even be talking about the '63 team if we hadn't beaten Army."

Ranked No. 2, the Mids accepted a bid to match with No. 1 Texas in the Cotton Bowl on New Year's Day. But the enormity of defeating the Longhorns while playing the role of America's sweetheart for a grieving nation proved impossible. Texas manhandled Navy, 28–6, and just like that, the greatest season in the Academy's history was over.

The next season, the optimism that surrounded Navy with Staubach returning evaporated almost immediately. Staubach badly injured his ankle and Achilles tendon in a 21–8 win at Penn State, and the injury lingered all season. Navy went 0-5-1 during a six-game stretch in the middle of the season and ended up 3-6-1 after an 11–8 loss to Army at the newly named JFK Stadium in Philadelphia. "I can't tell you why the 1964 season failed. It just wasn't good," Hardin said. "I have to take as much blame as the kids. We won together and we lost together, and that was how it ended."

It ended badly for Hardin, too. In Clary's *Navy Football*, Hardin had devised a ruse to try and win the 1964 Army game by telling his players it would be his last game. It caught Captain Bill Busik, Navy's athletic director, completely off-guard. When Busik asked if it was indeed his last game, Hardin replied, "It could be." Busik refused to permit the ruse, and Hardin's sharp tongue had collided with Academy leadership for the last time. The week following the Army game, Busik convened the athletic board and fired Hardin without a single objection.

Kennedy was gone. Erdelatz and Hardin were fired. Bellino and Staubach had graduated. Camelot was over. Without knowing it, a long, cold winter settled on the Navy program. It would last almost forty years.

## Chapter 2

# A LONG WINTER

## 1964–1994

Coming off an appearance in the Cotton Bowl and a 9-2 record, and with a Heisman Trophy winner returning at quarterback, Roger Staubach's senior season at Navy was a clunker. No one could have foreseen the way Navy limped through the 1964 season. Staubach couldn't stay healthy—part of a rash of forty players going down at various parts of the season—and the Mids stumbled to a 3-6-1 finish.

After firing Hardin, the Academy started stacking losing seasons like bad lottery tickets. Bill Elias took the reins in 1965. He went 15-22-3 over four seasons, a stark contrast to Hardin's 35-16-1. Elias's best season, a 5-4-1 mark in 1967, was almost identical to Hardin's worst season, a 5-5 record in 1962.

Next up was Rick Forzano, who returned to Navy in 1969 after spending a year under Paul Brown and the Cincinnati Bengals. He had also previously been head coach at the University of Connecticut, where he was a meager 7-10-1. An assistant coach under Hardin from 1959 to 1964, Forzano's appointment was not recommended by Brown, a mentor whose legendary career cannot be overstated. Instead, Brown thought Forzano should wait until a head coaching spot opened in the NFL.

But so smitten with Navy was Forzano, he couldn't turn the offer down. His four seasons in Annapolis were abysmal. He won just ten games against thirty-three losses and went a combined 2-8 against Army, Air Force and Notre Dame. No one doubted Forzano's deep and abiding respect for the Academy, its mission and methods. He had been a dynamite recruiter as an assistant coach—responsible for recruiting Navy stars like Tom Lynch, Pat Donnelly and Staubach—and was regarded as an outstanding position coach, too. But his tenure as head coach didn't translate into many wins. "He was so caught up in his love for the mystique of the Naval Academy that he believed he could replicate his prior experiences," said L. Budd Thalman, Navy's sports information director. "He reveled in coaching the Army-Navy game, in being around dedicated young men, and he was someone who really believed in the 'God and Country' concept."[10]

After going 17-43-1 in two collegiate stops, Brown's hopes of Forzano being an NFL head coach were, at best, remote. But after resigning from Navy on February 1, 1973, Forzano was offered and accepted an assistant coach position with the Detroit Lions. Brown was proven prophetic via an unimaginable and unforeseeable tragedy. Two days before the 1974 preseason opener, Lions head coach Don McCafferty died of a heart attack. Owner William Clay Ford promoted Forzano to head coach.

Forzano lasted a little more than two years. Four games into the 1976 season, with a locker room mutiny on his hands—not all of his making—Forzano was fired, although with a professional record of 15-17, it represented a marked improvement over his collegiate resume.

Forzano's stint with the Lions was his last notable position in football. He went on to embark on a very successful sales career in the Detroit auto industry. Always able to sell the deal, delivery was Forzano's only hiccup, at least as a head coach. An aside to the Forzano years: In 1975, Ted Marchibroda hired an aspiring college graduate for a preseason camp position with the Baltimore Colts. The next season, Forzano offered this same apprentice a full-time coaching position with the Lions. This young man was named Bill Belichick. In the off-season, Belichick brought his love and knowledge of lacrosse, then a niche, regional game limited to the Eastern seaboard, to Detroit Country Day, the well-to-do Detroit suburban high school that prepped future NBA stars Chris Webber and Shane Battier.

The sun finally came out for Navy when it hired George Welsh in February 1973. After graduating in 1955, Welsh spent seven years in the Navy, retired from active service and became an assistant coach under Rip Engle at Penn State. For fifteen largely unceremonious seasons, Engle led the Nittany Lions, including the first two years Welsh spent in coaching. But in 1965, a bolt of lightning arrived at Penn State in the form of Joe Paterno.

"Paterno had his hands in everything we did at Penn State….He was very involved in the defense, the offense, the quarterbacking, and he was obsessed with the running game," Welsh said, "and he was a fabulous recruiter. He not only knew who to recruit; he knew how to close. I learned a lot from watching Joe go into a house and close a kid and his parents on Penn State."

Almost immediately, Penn State went from a sleepy, parochial program to a national powerhouse, and Welsh immersed himself in the massive culture change. "Joe had a gift, one that couldn't be taught," Welsh said. "You either have it or you don't, and Joe had the 'it factor' more than any coach I ever worked with. I loved him."

But early in 1973, Welsh was interested in Princeton, and the Tigers were interested in him. During the second week of February, he interviewed for the job and thought he had a good chance to be offered. However, athletic officials were steadfast about not making an offer until the end of the month. It would be a huge mistake. "I hadn't solicited the job; [Princeton] had asked me to interview," Welsh said. "I was surprised by this disclosure." Just a few days later, Navy asked Welsh to come down to Annapolis. Athletic Director Bo Coppedge offered the job to Welsh on the spot, and he accepted.

Navy had enjoyed just one winning season between 1963 and Welsh's first season in 1973. But in nine years under Welsh, the Midshipmen went to three bowl games and earned their first nine-win season (1978) in fifteen years. It's been thirty-six years since Welsh left Annapolis accomplished and confident, bound for the same position at the University of Virginia. It was a far cry from how he arrived. "I didn't apply, because I wasn't sure I was ready, frankly. I'd only been an assistant coach, and a position coach, for six or seven years," Welsh said. "Penn State had a lot of influence on me, and most of it comes from Paterno. He had a lot of energy and a real knack—a gift—for football."

Bringing the best of Paterno's team to Annapolis, Welsh reconstructed a program that had won just twenty-eight games in the ten seasons since the 1964 Cotton Bowl, including just two wins against Army. At a time when the American military might have been at the lowest point in its history, Welsh recruited some of the most talented players in program history to the Academy. Broadcast interviews from Vietnam revealed GIs executing an internal revolt against the mission of the war. Massive protests of the Vietnam War were commonplace back home. President Richard Nixon was searching desperately for a way to leave Southeast Asia and achieve "Victory with Honor."

On top of those challenges, Welsh inherited a schedule that no first-year head coach would see today: four schools in the Top 20: No. 1 Notre Dame, No. 5 Penn State, No. 6 Michigan and No. 20 Tulane. After a pair of 4-7 seasons against schedules better suited for a national title contender, Welsh's

1975 team went 7-4, including a pair of one-point losses, at Washington and Georgia Tech. A win against either likely would have landed the Midshipmen into a bowl game.

A six-game losing streak sunk the 1976 team (4-7) and 1977 wasn't much better (5-6), but Welsh was beating Air Force and Army, the schools you're hired to beat in Annapolis. He was 4-1 against Army, winning the first four games by a combined 138–16 count, and his 3-2 mark against Air Force included two blowouts.

"We only won four games in three of the first four years, but we were playing Notre Dame, Penn State, Michigan, Syracuse, Georgia Tech, Pitt… the schedule was incredibly difficult," Welsh said. "I inherited some good players, more than I inherited at Virginia.…We struggled to recruit the first two or three years there. The core of the team the next three years was already there when I arrived, and they were tough."

By 1978, the rose was blooming on the flowers Welsh and his staff planted through five years of recruiting. Phil McConkey, an outstanding receiver who would play six seasons in the NFL and win the Super Bowl with the 1986 New York Giants, led the Mids to a 9-3 mark in 1978. The highlight of the year was a come-from-behind 23–16 win over BYU in the inaugural Holiday Bowl, the first bowl since Navy played Texas for the national title fifteen years earlier.

In Welsh's last four seasons, the Mids won thirty-one games and went to three bowls. Eight- and nine-win seasons have become almost commonplace under Johnson and Niumatalolo, but Welsh's success came against schedules comparable to a Big Ten or ACC slate now.

Schools like Pitt, Michigan, Notre Dame and Georgia Tech were regulars on Navy's schedule and, in most years, were national title contenders, too. Welsh recruited Eddie Meyers and Napoleon McCallum, arguably two of the greatest backs in Navy history, even if neither of them won a Heisman Trophy. "We came close to beating Michigan a couple times, but my two best teams were in 1975 and 1978, and both years, they weren't on our schedule," Welsh said of Coach Bo Schembechler's powerhouse program in Ann Arbor. "Overall, we played very well against Michigan and Notre Dame. Those games were always either at Michigan Stadium, Notre Dame Stadium or some NFL stadium in Cleveland, Baltimore or the Meadowlands in New Jersey. Those are tough games for a service academy to play."

When he left for Virginia in 1982, he owned a 6-3 ledger versus Air Force, a 7-1-1 mark against Army and an overall record of 55-46-1. He arrived at the Naval Academy position facing a massive rebuilding job and was leaving as Navy's winningest coach.

Welsh's record stood as the all-time mark at Navy until December 13, 2014, when Niumatalolo earned his fifty-sixth victory, a 17–10 win over Army in Baltimore. The difference was Niumatalolo had the advantage of assuming a team already at full steam, while Welsh had to build the kind of program he had played within more than twenty years earlier—and from the ground up.

Welsh left…and the chill quickly returned. Gary Tranquill, a former Welsh assistant, took the helm. He also spent time on staff at Ohio State and West Virginia before coming back to Annapolis. Tranquill wasn't walking into a rebuilding project. He was taking over a team with a winning percentage of .670 the past four seasons and a Heisman Trophy candidate on the roster. As a freshman, Napoleon McCallum had taken a limited number of snaps behind Meyers.

Tranquill went 6-5 in 1982 before driving the program right back off the cliff, going 14-29-1 the next four seasons. Compounding the poor record was the fact McCallum was an All-American in 1983 and, after breaking his ankle in the second game of 1984, was granted the rare opportunity to apply to the NCAA for a fifth year of eligibility. The hopeful enthusiasm for 1985 never materialized in a 4-7 season.

Tranquill was a respectable 3-2 versus Army, but he was 0-5 against Air Force. Welsh dominated the service rivalries and left a full cupboard for an assistant who was part of the rebuilding, and all that came of it was twenty wins in fifty-five tries—a .373 winning percentage. Just thirteen of those wins came against Division I schools.

As Dave Sell of the *Washington Post* noted, the 1986 Mids lost badly on a few occasions and were beaten by I-AA schools Penn and Delaware. After his final game, a 27-7 drubbing by Army, he was fired. Tranquill told the *Post*, "I don't feel like [a win Saturday] would have made any difference." Coppedge had already received word from NAAA's board of directors to pass on renewing Tranquill's contract. Less than twenty-four hours after losing to the Cadets, Tranquill was out.

Sell's article made significant mention of the "strict academic and military demands" as a "major reason service academy teams have struggled." Had the climate surrounding Academy football really changed that much in just five years? No, but major college football was changing, evolving from a business built largely on ticket revenues, parking and concession sales to one on the doorstep of the massive television contract rights era and major licensing revenues from shirts, jerseys and personal seat licenses in the form of donations to the school. This capital infusion would fuel an arms race, one that Navy was ill-equipped to fight much less win.

Next up was Elliot Uzelac, also a former Navy assistant, pried away after six years on Schembechler's Michigan staff, for the 1987 season. The prevailing hope was that Uzelac could implement the best of the Michigan program, as Welsh had done fifeen years earlier. Uzelac had previously spent seven seasons as head coach at Western Michigan from 1975 to 1981, going 38-39, but had posted five winning seasons in his last six after opening at 1-10 in 1975.

If Navy thought it struggled under Tranquill, Uzelac quickly made him look like Vince Lombardi. In three seasons, Uzelac won just three Division I games—North Carolina, Boston College and Army—and all in 1989, his final season. His 8-25 record included a 5-5 mark versus the various I-AA schools populating Navy's schedule. With a fourth year left on his contract, Uzelac became the first coach in Academy history to be fired after beating Army, and the decision left him salty: "We beat Army, I come in for the team function and I get fired. It's been a helluva day," Uzelac told the *Washington Post*.

Navy Athletic Director Jack Lengyel justified Uzelac's dismissal by saying he didn't think an evaluation meeting would be anything more than a formality. There had been significant warning signs. Following the end of the 1988 season, Uzelac's inconsistent wishbone offense forced an internal discussion about potentially switching to a pro-set offense. Lengyel confirmed as much in the *Post*'s story announcing Uzelac's dismissal, saying, "Those concerns were shared a year ago.…It's the coach's responsibility to accept or reject them, or at least be aware of them."

Stories populated from anonymous sources within the athletic department told of the groundswell that drove Uzelac out at Navy. Alumni canceling season ticket accounts and his lack of popularity among prominent Academy officials were most popular. "The frustration [with Uzelac] is that we're a leadership institution, and in the evaluation of the last three years, we feel the program hasn't portrayed the leadership commensurate with the standards of the United States Naval Academy," Lengyel said in a *Washington Post* story by Anthony Cotton from December 12, 1989. Indignant, Uzelac denied it, saying, "I just know that I didn't do anything to embarrass the academy."[11]

But Lengyel's comments were underscored when Uzelac, who spent 1990 as an offensive line coach at Indiana, landed on John Cooper's staff at Ohio State in 1991. Almost immediately, he was outed by former Buckeye and future

Minnesota Viking running back Robert Smith for encouraging and pressuring players to skip class so they could make practice. In protest, Smith, a premed student who was named the United Press International (UPI) Freshman of the Year in 1990, quit the team on August 23, just eight days into fall camp. On September 9, *Sports Illustrated* ran a story titled "Goodbye, Columbus" detailing an account from an anonymous Midshipmen who accused Uzelac of the same tactics to prioritize football over school at Navy:

> *A former midshipman who played for Uzelac at Navy recalls that Uzelac discouraged players from enrolling in summer-school courses that conflicted with workouts during two-a-days. Said the former Middie, "If a guy who'd been in class that morning screwed up in the afternoon, [Uzelac] would say, 'You're sitting in a classroom all morning when you could have been out here doing drill work!'"*

Ohio State forced Uzelac's resignation on February 21, 1992, and Smith returned to the team that fall.

Entering the 1990s, securing a fourth coach in ten years was only part of the problems Navy faced. Air Force's success on the field, which including beating programs like Ohio State and Notre Dame, and the success the school was enjoying in recruiting and securing postseason games, was forcing the two East Coast military academies to reconsider how they sustained their programs. "Because we were never going to overcome the interest in that [Army-Navy] game, we had to be different than Army and Navy," former Air Force coach Fisher DeBerry said. "We needed something to separate us. Our conference membership and triple-option offense was the difference-maker for us."

Air Force's option offense was mitigating talent deficiencies and positively exposing the program's brand on television and in bowl games. As a member of the Western Athletic Conference, Air Force was playing for conference titles, giving the Falcons a huge boost in recruiting. It was thought that Army and Navy should follow.

Karl Benson, running the Mid-American Conference (MAC) as a nine-school conference in the early 1990s, recalled the discussion about Army and Navy joining the conference. "There was hesitation on both sides," Benson said. "One, Army and Navy had built a legacy as independents, so they weren't going to give that up—and share the money they generated—unless it was an opportunity that benefited them greatly....At the same time, they were struggling to win consistently, and I think they would have found some really great success in the MAC. Would I have loved to have Army-Navy as a MAC conference game? Absolutely."

Benson transformed the MAC into a football conference before leaving for the Western Athletic Conference in 1994. "I'm the guy they always blame for ruining MAC basketball," Benson said with a laugh, but he couldn't sway the MAC's presidents, athletic directors or coaches to share the MAC's one precious advantage: proximity. The conference headquarters in Toledo, Ohio, was just two hundred miles away from any of the member schools in Michigan, Ohio and Indiana. "We had a proposal to join from Northern Illinois University to join the MAC, but our membership viewed DeKalb, Ill., as a western outpost," Benson said. "We were struggling to sell our membership on NIU. Selling them on Annapolis and West Point was impossible."

The MAC eventually added Akron, to get to ten, before Marshall and later Buffalo joined. There was a dalliance with Temple and Massachusetts, too. The MAC would eventually settle in as a twelve-school league. Army joined Conference USA in 1998 with unspectacular results, and Air Force merged into the Mountain West. Navy decided to remain independent, a decision Vice Admiral John Ryan, Superintendent at the Academy from 1998 to 2002, described as one of the best decisions Navy ever made. "[Conference USA] tried like hell to get Navy to go into that.…They offered us everything but the kitchen sink…but we said, 'No thank you,'" Ryan said. "Not going into Conference USA really set us up for success later on."

Lengyel tabbed George Chaump, who wanted to run a pro-set offense, as his new coach. Chaump won the job over candidates like Charlie Taaffe (The Citadel), Jimmye Laycock (William and Mary) and Gene Stallings (Arizona Cardinals, Alabama). He had compiled a 33-16-1 mark at Marshall, where Lengyel had coached after the infamous plane crash in 1970.

Chaump thought he could recruit with the powerful legacy schools, which routinely gobble up the best pro-set prospects. To no one's surprise, that didn't happen. And dumbing down the schedule didn't help much, either. A 5-6 mark in 1990 was artificially inflated by wins against I-AA schools Richmond, Villanova and Delaware, but in 1991 and 1992, Chaump's Mids suffered through consecutive 1-10 seasons, going 0-3 versus I-AA schools, too. Worse, Navy didn't score until the fourth quarter of the fourth game in 1992 and lost five quarterbacks while doing it.

Academy leadership should have cut Chaump loose after 1992 but inexplicably retained him for two more unspectacular seasons. While the

Mids finally broke an eleven-game losing streak to Air Force with a 28–24 win in 1993, they won just seven of eighteen games in 1993 and 1994.

Chaump was fired on Sunday, December 4, 1994, the day after losing his fourth game to Army in five tries. He dodged media requests while cleaning out his desk. It was just as well; his 14-41 record spoke plenty for him.

Just as with Tranquill's dismissal, significant mention was made of post-graduation military commitment and stringent academic standards hampering the Academy's football program, this time in Alan Goldstein's article in the *Baltimore Sun*: "Chaump experienced mostly frustration at the academy, where stringent academic standards and a six-year service commitment after graduation proved major obstacles in recruiting gifted athletes. 'At Marshall, I could go after football players, get them in school and keep them there,' Chaump said recently."[12]

The Academy's mission or methods hadn't been a problem for Erdelatz, Hardin or Welsh. Attracting top-flight talent who could handle the academic rigor was a task coaches faced at other schools, like Duke, Stanford and Northwestern. No, Navy was failing despite some outstanding talent, some of All-American caliber. But when these coaches failed to deliver the one metric that matters—wins—blame shifted to excuses aside from the obvious problem.

Elias and Forzano had gone a combined 25-55-3, a miserable .322 winning percentage from 1965 to 1973. Tranquill, Uzelac and Chaump followed with a 44-100-1 mark from 1982 to 1994, a .306 percentage. In the twenty-one years bookending George Welsh, five coaches managed just fourteen more victories than Welsh (who had to rebuild the program completely) won in eight seasons (fifty-five).

The only mission Jack Lengyel had to execute was finding a coach who could recruit enough talent to win consistently. He would find that man in Utah, but it wouldn't stop the wolves from within the Department of Defense and federal legislature from growling at the Academy's gate.

Chapter 3

# AIR FORCE

**M**ore than any other fact, one dominates Navy's fifteen-year renaissance under Johnson and Niumatalolo: It doesn't happen without Air Force. The success of the Falcons drove Navy to finally say "enough."

Over twenty-eight seasons at three schools, Ken Niumatalolo has seen Air Force more than anyone else at Navy, so he knows the intensity swirling around the game with the Falcons better than anyone else. "If Army is the game you're at Navy to win, Air Force is the game you cannot lose," Niumatalolo said of the Falcons, a team that has been on every schedule he's ever played or coached, a list that includes Hawaii, Navy, UNLV and Navy again, dating back to the late 1980s. "As important as Army is, there's euphoria when you beat Air Force and heartbreak when you lose."

The Air Force game will never be bigger than Army, but most of major college football's media or fans don't realize how much the first week of October means to Navy. It lacks the media's run-up of pageantry and valor that oozes over Army-Navy, but Navy–Air Force is a must-see game filled with acrimony. Oh yeah, and the winner of the Navy–Air Force game has won or retained the CIC Trophy the last twenty years. There's that, too.

"Playing Navy in the fourth or fifth game of the season, the game becomes so much bigger because the goal of winning the CIC is tied so closely to winning the Navy game," DeBerry said. "Win it and your season takes on a much bigger importance. Lose it and your season takes a big dive. That's one of the big reasons the rivalry is what it is."

And then there's the recruiting battles. Jeff Monken, who helped rebuild the Navy program under Johnson and is now head coach at Army, says no game simmers with animosity like Air Force. "The rivalry comes more from the things [Air Force] says and does away from that game…in recruiting, and in the media.…It gives the rivalry that salty taste," Monken said. "The game certainly doesn't get the attention that others do but they do plenty of stuff outside of the 60 minutes of time you're out there against them one time a year that gets you fired up enough to want to beat them."

Keenan Reynolds, who went 3-1 versus the Falcons, and was heavily recruited by Air Force, says: "Straight-up, flat-out, it's a really bitter rivalry. We just don't like each other. There's a lot of running jokes about Air Force, how they don't do anything in the military, the whole 'Chair Force' thing. But there's something about that game. It really stings when you don't win."

The disdain for Air Force starts on the recruiting trails, at least as far as Army and Navy are concerned. Many of the players populating the Navy roster were recruited by at least one of the other two service academies.

Is the likelihood of being killed in action as an infantryman in the U.S. Army or as a ground forces marine in the U.S. Navy greater than the chances of being killed in the U.S. Air Force? Do naval officers suffer higher divorce rates as compared to the Air Force? Is the suicide rate at one academy higher than at the others? Monken said some of the negative tactics Air Force has used begs a bigger question: should those questions be put in front of prospective student athletes at any service academy?

"When I was at Navy, our admissions liaison pulled stuff out of a book and told us, 'Here's what Air Force sends to our guys.' It was divorce rates in the Navy as compared to the Air Force…things like that," Monken said. "You want to recruit that way? Fine. It works for them, and they probably win more of the battles because of it. And frankly, they recruit and say, 'It's easier here. You don't have to do this and you don't have to do that.' I'm not sure all of it is completely truthful, but it is what it is."

To be fair to current Air Force coach Troy Calhoun and his staff, the claim of negative recruiting tactics is common among major college football rivals. It's a highly competitive, alpha-dog business, and what separates schools from one another on the football field comes from recruiting. Calhoun refused multiple requests for comment on recruiting or any of his team's success.

This is the theater that surrounds the game between the Falcons and Midshipmen. I discovered it in 2009 when, after moving from Michigan to Maryland, I pined for the build-up to and excitement of a Big Ten game day.

That kind of fervor doesn't exist in College Park, Maryland, where Maryland was an Atlantic Coast Conference school until 2014 and has been a Big Ten school since. The Terrapins aren't anyone's true rival. Maryland has developed no significant rivals in football, and while there were some memorable basketball games between Duke and North Carolina, as much as Terrapin fans want it to be true, the Terps were not and are not true rivals with Tobacco Road's two heavyweights.

So, my attention turned toward Annapolis and Navy, for what I naïvely thought was a local, feel-good story. Navy had a big rivalry with Army, but it was a rivalry I knew nothing about, like Harvard and Yale. In that way, it's cliché. Everyone knows about Harvard-Yale or Army-Navy, but how many fans really know anything specific about those teams when they meet each year?

October 3, 2009, was a postcard-perfect kind of day in Annapolis. A warm, sunny sky oozed from above while my stepson Kyle and I watched Michigan State score an improbable touchdown on the last play to beat Michigan in overtime from the parking lot. Then we went into Navy–Marine Corps Memorial Stadium and watched Navy outlast Air Force in overtime, 16–13. When Air Force's thirty-one-yard field goal attempt sailed wide of the left upright on the game's last play, the contrasting scene on the two sidelines was the perfect snapshot of the rivalry's importance. The Falcons, after a seventh consecutive loss to Navy, crumbled like crushed beer cans. Navy's sideline erupted in joy when the kick missed. Of Navy's seven consecutive wins in the series to that point, six had been decided by one possession or less, and 2009 was the first overtime game.

After the two teams stood for each other's alma mater—because they won, Navy sang second—the entire Brigade of Midshipmen stood in anticipation while the rest of the crowd milled about. Everyone was waiting for one more big moment, and my son and I seemed to be the only ones who didn't know why. Then the stadium's public address crackled one more time, announcing the rarest of rewards: "Your attention, please: By order of the Commandant of the United States Naval Academy, in honor of tonight's victory, all Midshipmen are hereby granted…a full weekend liberty!"

The ensuing roar was the loudest of the night. Immediately, four thousand Midshipmen, clad in their summer whites, turned and started sprinting up the risers, headed out of the stadium and into downtown Annapolis at full steam. They filled dozens of restaurants and pubs down on the docks or spent the rest of the weekend at a sponsor parent's home, away from military uniform and weekend guard duty.

Fisher DeBerry led Air Force for twenty-three years, and his success pushed Navy to adapt their program to the triple-option under Charlie Weatherbie in 1995. *U.S. Air Force/Danny Meyer*.

Meanwhile, Air Force's locker room of Cadets was as quiet as a morgue. Answers to the media were related at little more than a whisper. "We're kind of demoralized, especially the seniors on the squad because they've never beaten this Navy team," Air Force quarterback Tim Jefferson told the Associated Press.

Navy previously knew the feeling well. From 1982 to 2002, Air Force owned the rivalry, beating the Midshipmen nineteen times in twenty-one games. While Navy struggled to remain relevant, Air Force was racking up wins, annually going to bowl games and dominating the CIC Trophy race.

The man primarily responsible for this success was Coach Fisher DeBerry, and he wore the black hat in Annapolis the same way Michael Jordan did as a villain in Detroit. DeBerry had a great program, and the Falcons didn't hide their pride. "We knew we weren't the big game for Army and Navy. Winning those academy games brought us great pleasure," DeBerry said. "If that was tough [for fans of Navy], well, we were focused on what we were trying to do."

What they were doing was winning the CIC Trophy fourteen times in DeBerry's first twenty years, while Navy was shut out completely from 1982 to 2002. "Our kids beat Notre Dame four straight times, but winning the CIC was the biggest deal on our schedule," DeBerry said. "The difference, until this year, was if Navy lost to Air Force, their No. 1 goal was gone. We had conference goals, we had Notre Dame and we had the CIC."

Making matters worse, Navy was trapped in a forty-three-game losing streak to Notre Dame. DeBerry's success with the triple-option offense factored heavily in Navy's decision to hire Charlie Weatherbie in 1995. Weatherbie's six years he had spent under DeBerry in Colorado Springs meant as much as the three seasons he spent as head coach at Utah State.

The rivalry Navy shares with Air Force and Army reminds one of the symbiotic relationship Michigan, Michigan State and Ohio State share in the Big Ten. If that sounds like an over-the-top comparison, consider the following: The three military rivals are Department of Defense academies just like the aforementioned Midwest heavyweights are Big Ten schools. Army and Navy, the two East Coast academies, are separated from Air Force in Colorado Springs, Colorado, the same way anyone from Michigan or Michigan State will tell you the state of Ohio is the worst place in the world, stated as fact. Navy first met Air Force in 1960; the Falcons didn't become an annual inclusion on both schedules until 1972. Similarly, Michigan State didn't join the Big Ten until 1950, when the Spartans' admission took the nastiness between the states of Michigan and Ohio to an entirely new level. Ohio State is Michigan's "must win" game, just like Army is Navy's primary rival, leaving a perfect "Little Brother" glaze over the Air Force game in the same way it washes over Michigan State's game with Michigan.

Finally, the Midshipmen don't play Air Force in all sports, so when it comes to bragging rights between the two academies, it starts and ends with the football game.

"The Navy game has become a lot like playing your brother," DeBerry said. "You have to see that school in the same recruiting circles, running the same offense and trying to accomplish the same goals."

Paul Johnson started dominating the series for Navy in 2003. Since then, celebration and heartbreak have earmarked every meeting. An abundance of classic finishes leaves each fan base circling the date of the next year's game in red.

It all turned in the Mids' favor in 2003, when Navy stunned No. 25 Air Force, 28–25, in Washington, D.C., their first win over a ranked opponent in eighteen seasons. The next year, Geoff Blumenfeld booted the Mids

In 2004, Navy's Geoff Blumenfeld gave Air Force the boot, kicking the game-winning field goal with four seconds left, lifting Navy past Air Force, 24–21, and giving the Mids' their first 5-0 start since 1979. *U.S. Air Force/Charley Starr.*

past the Falcons with a thirty-yard field goal on the last play of the game, stunning a crowd of 44,279 in Colorado Springs with a 24–21 win.

That was the year Johnson infamously said the Mids had "the worst kicking game in America" after missing four field goals and an extra point in their first four games. But he didn't miss a subtle shot at the Falcons after the game, either. "We know the trophy isn't coming back here," he said, referring to the six consecutive seasons Air Force won the CIC Trophy before losing it to Navy in 2003.[13]

Returning to Annapolis in 2005, Navy trailed, 24–17, and after taking the football with 4:26 left in the game, faced a fourth-down conversion from their twenty-nine. The Midshipmen converted and, three plays later, hit Reggie Campbell with a forty-yard strike to tie with 2:22 left. When Air Force failed to convert a first down, they shanked a punt just nine yards.

With no timeouts and the clock ticking down, Navy's kicking team rushed onto the field, hurrying furiously to snap the football. Joe Bullen set for an instant and then moved forward with four-tenths of a second on the stadium clock to blister a career-long forty-six-yarder.

"It's good!" Brian Hampton (3) knows as Joey Bullen (39) watches his game-winning field goal pass through the goal posts with 0:00.4 left in a dramatic 27–24 win over Air Force. The Falcons' Carson Bird (2) rolls over and out of the play. *U.S. Navy/Damon J. Moritz.*

*Right*: Joey Bullen kicks off the party following a game-winning field goal to beat Air Force 27–24 in 2005. *U.S. Navy/Damon J. Moritz*.

*Below*: Navy runs toward the Brigade of Midshipmen to sing second, an honor for defeating Air Force 27–24 in 2005. *U.S. Navy/Damon J. Moritz*.

Navy had stolen a 27–24 decision, the third consecutive three-point win in the series. The Falcons were despondent. "The goals of our program are gone," Air Force quarterback Shaun Carney told the *Baltimore Sun*'s Kent Baker.[14]

The rivalry reached a bitter crescendo in 2006 after Navy's 24–17 win. In the post-game press conference, Johnson declared himself "proud to be the coach of the luckiest team in America" before detailing how his Midshipmen chafed at reading about Air Force players reportedly describing recent losses to Navy as "embarrassing." In the same Associated Press story, DeBerry denied the comments, saying, "[Johnson] didn't hear it from my football team."

It was DeBerry's last appearance in the rivalry. He retired with three years and $2.5 million left on a contract that paid him $770,000 per year. The year before, DeBerry's comments about "needing to recruit more Afro-Americans" following a 48–10 loss to TCU earned him a reprimand from the Academy and forced him to make a public apology.

Those comments, and a mini-controversy about religious intones printed on a banner inside Air Force's locker room, hounded DeBerry at every press conference since, but it was the three straight losing seasons and his loosening grip on the CIC Trophy that took the biggest toll.

DeBerry left Air Force with a 169-109-1 record. His twenty-three years was third-longest at one school, behind Penn State's Joe Paterno (41) and Florida State's Bobby Bowden (31). That Air Force still owns a 29-20 advantage in the series remains attributable to DeBerry. "When you lose to an opponent you want to beat and need to beat and you're recruiting against those schools," DeBerry said, "it really takes a lot of juice out of you."

Calhoun took over in Colorado Springs in 2007, while Niumatalolo took the wheel in Annapolis late that same season. By this time, media was starting to recognize how Air Force was eclipsing Army in importance and drama for Navy. In a 2008 story about Navy's 33–27 win over the Falcons, the *Washington Post*'s Camille Powell noted that while Navy–Air Force might not receive the kind of national attention that Army-Navy does, it has produced better and more meaningful games.[15]

In that victory, the Mids blocked two Air Force punts for touchdowns. Blake Carter ran one blocked punt back twenty-five yards for a score and later blocked a rugby-style kick that Navy recovered in the end zone for another touchdown. It was Navy's twelfth straight win over a service rival, tying Air Force's mark from 1997 to 2002.

U.S. Air Force's Kyle Lumpkin eludes Navy's Ram Vela (34), but the Falcons couldn't escape a sixth straight loss to Navy, 33–27, in 2008. *U.S. Air Force/Rachel Boettcher.*

The fabulous theater followed in 2009. After Joe Buckley booted a thirty-eight-yarder on the first possession of overtime to put Navy up, 16–13, Air Force's Eric Soderberg pulled his thirty-one-yard try left of the upright. This is what the rivalry had become: an annual celebration for the Mids and heartbreak for the Falcons. From 2003 to 2009, only one game was decided by more than seven points. Navy wasn't blowing the Falcons out like it was rolling over Army. Just a handful of plays and 35 points—an average margin of victory of 5.1 per game—separated Air Force from seven years of frustration.

Calhoun and the Falcons finally broke through in 2010, eking out a 14–6 win in Colorado by blocking a punt and holding Dobbs without a touchdown for the first time in seventeen career starts. It was Navy's first loss in a service rival game after fifteen straight wins. "It was a monkey off [Calhoun's] back and a monkey off my back. I wanted to beat Navy just as bad as anyone else out here," Jefferson told the Associated Press.

The next year, controversy made for one of the more memorable finishes in the rivalry's history. Air Force commanded a 28–10 lead into the fourth quarter before the Midshipmen staged a final, frenetic ten-minute rally. Jon Teague's field goal and a pair of touchdowns by quarterback Kriss

Navy's Emmett Merchant (7), Ram Vela (34), Ross Pospisil (51) and Tyler Simmons (54) slam the brakes on Air Force's Jared Tew during the Mids' 16–13 overtime win in 2009. *U.S. Navy/Oscar Sosa.*

Proctor—a seven-yard run and a five-yard pass to Gee Gee Greene—set the stage for the dramatic two-point conversion try with nineteen seconds left. When Alexander Teich barreled across the goal line, the partisan Annapolis crowd was delirious. Improbably, the game was going to overtime tied at twenty-eight.

Navy kept momentum with the first possession in overtime, when Proctor bulled his way in from a yard out to give Navy a 34–28 lead. But while celebrating before the extra point, Proctor was hit with a fifteen-yard unsportsmanlike conduct foul. Forcing Navy to kick from thirty-five yards out allowed Air Force's Alex Means to block the PAT, and suddenly, the Falcons were staring at the same joy a bank robber feels looking at an open vault full of money without a police officer in sight.

After the Falcons' Tim Jefferson scored, Air Force quickly booted the extra point to steal a 35–34 victory, leaving Navy enraged. Teich was so distraught he walked off the field before the playing of Air Force's alma mater, a huge honor code violation.

In his story for the Associated Press, David Ginsberg described Niumatalolo and Proctor as "furious," while Teich called the foul

Tim Jefferson's touchdown in overtime in 2011 gave Air Force a 35–34 win and capped one of the most controversial finishes in the rivalry's history. *U.S. Air Force/ Russ Scalf.*

Air Force fans celebrate the game-winning score in the Falcons' 35–34 success in overtime in 2011. *U.S. Air Force/Russ Scalf.*

"pitiful." Proctor explained his actions: "I got up and started to head to our sideline. Some guy got in my way and I said, 'Move.' Then [the] referee made the call."

There was just one problem: video didn't support Proctor's assertion, and an op-ed in the *Capital-Gazette* the next week said as much: "Proctor leapt to his feet after scoring and made a noticeable, two-handed push into Air Force defensive lineman Nick DeJulio. Proctor then bounded to the opposite end of the clustered players and crashed his facemask into defensive back Jon Davis' ear hole. It's impossible not to notice Proctor forcibly turning himself in to Davis while saying something. Proctor wasn't looking for the bench but instead, looking for something to say to his opponents."[16]

That's when the flag was thrown. As much as the loss made Navy's teeth itch in the days following the game, after coaches had time to review and digest the play, the controversy died down considerably. Niumatalolo, to his credit, was only upset the flag helped decide the game. He knew why officials threw the flag and couldn't deny the unsportsmanlike actions of his quarterback. The question was, did the penalty *really* fit the crime? Niumatalolo thought, "Don't the officials know how important the Air Force game is to us?"

Still, a violation is a violation, and Navy stripped Teich, a senior, of his captaincy and suspended him for the next game, too. The controversy also revealed Proctor's character, or possible lack thereof, and it wouldn't be the last time. Just days away from being commissioned the following May, Proctor made headlines when it was learned he was resigning from the U.S. Navy. Two months earlier, he was caught cheating on a thermodynamics quiz. Rather than fight the honor code violation and face the very real possibility of separation, he agreed to voluntarily pay back approximately $160,000 of tuition and resign.

Proctor's honor code case was in the early stages of a review process that typically begins with peer remediation and works through several steps, potentially all the way up to the Pentagon. Commander William Marks told the *Baltimore Sun* the case was considered serious but that it was not clear whether he would have been dismissed from the Academy.[17] Proctor didn't hide from his wrongdoing in the same 2012 article, admitting that he wasn't committed to a naval career.

Losing the Air Force game two years in a row is a gut punch, and Navy needed to respond. It would take a roll of the dice by Niumatalolo that allowed the legend of Keenan Reynolds to be born in the 2012 game. Niumatalolo put Reynolds, an untested plebe, into a firestorm with the Mids trailing,

21–13, in the fourth quarter. Reynolds drove the Mids down for a fifteen-yard touchdown and then overcame a near-disastrous decision to pitch the ball on the ensuing two-point conversion when Noah Copeland avoided a tackle in the backfield and dove inside the pylon to tie the score. After Jake Zuzek recovered Reynolds's fumble in the end zone for a touchdown and Wes Henderson batted down a fourth-down pass on Air Force's last play, Navy had improbably won in overtime.

The story in 2013 was the federal government sequestration—media described it as a "shutdown"—that jeopardized the game, as all non-essential spending by the Department of Defense was halted. Just days before the game, the sequestration ended, and the cost of the charter taking the Falcons into Baltimore was picked up by USAA. The game went off without a hitch, although Air Force probably wishes it never played at all.

Navy striker linebacker C.J. Johnson, who previously suffered two catastrophic ACL injuries, made eight tackles and intercepted quarterback Karson Roberts twice on national television in front of the largest crowd ever at Navy–Marine Corps Memorial Stadium. "Playing that well in such a huge game of that magnitude on national TV, that doesn't happen often," Johnson said in a *Capital Gazette* story profiling his career a year later. "That was a dream game come true."[18]

Keenan Reynolds dives across the goal line in the 2014 Air Force game, won by the Falcons, 31–20. *U.S. Navy/EJ Hersom.*

The Falcons handed Reynolds his only loss to a service rival in 2014 when Kale Pearson hit Garrett Brown with a touchdown pass with thirty-five seconds left to seal a 31–20 win. Air Force held Navy to just thirty-six rushing yards in the second half.

Reynolds left the rivalry on a high note, rushing for 183 yards as Navy took a 21–0 lead into halftime en route to a 33–11 blowout in Annapolis in 2015.

A year later, Navy flew into Colorado Springs undefeated after four games. A win would have potentially brought ESPN's *College GameDay* show to Annapolis for a battle of unbeatens with Houston the following weekend. True to the rivalry, Air Force spoiled those plans with a 28–14 win that wasn't as close as the final score indicated. Tim McVey's 62-yard touchdown sealed a dominant performance by the Falcons, who racked up 430 yards of total offense.

The next week, Navy pulled off the biggest upset of the 2016 season, thanks to Admiral Bill Byrne, a former Navy quarterback. "Adm. Byrne was talking to some families for Second Class Parents Weekend when coach Niumatalolo called him over," said Will Worth. "He gave an impromptu speech about how in his day, they had just lost to Notre Dame, 18–17, and they bounced back with a huge win over No. 2 South Carolina. I think from that point on, we had the confidence and energy to do it."

The next Saturday, Navy stunned No. 6 Houston, 46–40. Still, the sting of losing to Air Force remained. "There's something about those guys…you hate to lose to them," Worth said. "There's a bitter feeling to it, especially when we go out to Colorado and lose on their turf…it makes for a long flight home."

Chapter 4

# THE BIG TEASE

## 1995–2001

Since 2003, Navy has won more than in any other era of the program's history. Entering 2017, the Midshipmen are 121-61 (.664) since December 7, 2002, when they overwhelmed Army, 58–12. The fourteen consecutive wins over Army was the apex of the incredible, improbable resurrection of a program.

Before that, Navy football wasn't just dormant—it was on the doorstep of Division I death, having managed a meager 73-158-1 record (.316) from 1982 until that 2002 Army game. In 2001, an Academy-sponsored review of the athletic department recommended the program step down to I-AA or FCS status.

So, what does any of this have to do with 1995? To say the rebirth of the program started in 2002 under Paul Johnson isn't entirely correct. The seeds of the last fifteen years were planted by Charlie Weatherbie.

Hired in 1995 and fired with three games remaining in 2001, Weatherbie's tenure lasted seven years and seventy-five games. He started spectacularly, marching Navy to twenty-one wins in his first thirty-four games and earning the program's first bowl win in eighteen years. His finish was a disaster, as Navy lost seventeen of the last eighteen and twenty of twenty-one overall. He was mercifully fired the day after a 21–20 loss at Toledo on October 27, 2001.

No one in Annapolis disputes the ending: Weatherbie had to go. But the success in his first three seasons whet the appetite for football again in Annapolis. Twenty years later, the story has become about Navy's dramatic rise to reclaim its former status as an iconic brand within America's greatest spectator sport, and 1995 is when it started.

To appreciate Navy's renaissance, you must understand the abysmal results under Uzelac and Chaump from 1987 to 1994. Missteps plagued both, and neither could recruit the talent or implement the correct scheme needed to be successful. This was never more evident than the first three games of the 1992 season, when Navy lost by a combined score of 121–0 and the Midshipmen had five different quarterbacks injured in the process.

In 1993, six football players were implicated in an Academy-wide electrical engineering cheating scandal. Chaump and his assistants couldn't build depth fast enough, and Navy had no chance to out-recruit name-brand, Power 5 schools for the talent they needed. After going 5-6 in his first season, Chaump won just nine times over the next four years, and he was fired the day after a 22–20 loss to Army in Philadelphia.

Almost immediately, speculation ramped up regarding Chaump's replacement. The *Washington Post* mentioned Tom O'Brien, a 1971 Academy grad who coached at Navy under George Welsh in 1975–81 and then followed him to become his offensive coordinator at Virginia, as an early favorite to succeed him. Boston College defensive coordinator Steve Szabo and former Super Bowl champion quarterback Doug Williams (already a Navy assistant coach) were also mentioned as potential replacements.

O'Brien had been mentioned as a possible replacement in 1990, but he couldn't secure an interview. This time, O'Brien interviewed but didn't land the job. O'Brien understood the Academy better than any other candidate. But in his interview, military and athletic administrators were turned off by his blunt assessments of the state of the program. No one at Navy wanted to hear it.

An aside to the O'Brien dalliance: two years later, he would become the head coach at Boston College—a position offered first to Weatherbie three different times in December 1996—and go 4-1 against Navy. After trouncing the Mids, 46–21, in 2002, O'Brien scoffed publicly to the *Boston Globe* that Navy didn't play the 4-3 defensive scheme it listed in a weekly release: "I mean, you expect them to tell you who's going to play and who's not; that's common courtesy," O'Brien told the *Boston Globe*. "I guess the honor concept [at Navy] doesn't apply to the coaches."

O'Brien, who also made snarky comments about injuries his team took on while defending Navy's option offense, quickly backtracked. "I called him and he apologized," Johnson told the *Baltimore Sun*'s Kevin Van Valkenburg.

"He said he was out of line. I mean short of sending him practice tapes, I don't know what he wants....As far as the other comments about our offense, if I gave up 480 yards with that team I would be embarrassed, too."

Any bridges O'Brien had left in place at the Academy were rubble.

But in 1995, Weatherbie, with his slicked-back hair and ability to quote scripture, was a charismatic salesman who won over Lengyel and USNA's leadership. There was a certain level of naïveté during this era among leadership of the Academy. Military leaders weren't necessarily savvy to the game-changing nature of college athletics or taking orders from civilian athletic directors.

Three weeks later, Lengyel handed the job to Weatherbie, who had led Utah State for the last three years. He had gone 15-19 at Utah State, including leading the Aggies to their first winning season since 1980 and a bowl win over Ball State. Massive budget cuts had sabotaged Weatherbie's third season (3-8), but he had none of the advantages of a program like Navy, and facing a massive rebuilding job, all of it impressed Lengyel.

Weatherbie won the job based on his six-year stint as an assistant at Air Force and the modest success he enjoyed at Utah State. "In our selection process, you look at a man's total background," Lengyel told the *Baltimore Sun* in a December 31, 1995 article about the hiring. "Weatherbie has been successful at every level. He walks the walk."

With a five-year contract worth a reported $170,000 per year under his arm, Weatherbie began assembling a dynamic staff of assistant coaches worthy of any Power 5 school. Johnson was named offensive coordinator. Dick Bumpas had an outstanding reputation and was named defensive coordinator. Gary Patterson, who later ascended to head coach at Texas Christian, came aboard under Bumpas, and Johnson brought his protégé, a young, Polynesian ball of fire named Ken Niumatalolo.

After a 5-6 record in 1995, Navy rocketed to a 9-3 record in 1996 that included wins over Georgia Tech, Wake Forest and Air Force. A heartbreaking 28–24 loss to Army in Philadelphia aside, the Midshipmen earned victory over Steve Mariucci's California Bears in the Aloha Bowl, 42–38, played on Christmas Day in Honolulu. "The first year, we probably should have won 3 or 4 more games, and then we were 9-3 the next year, and probably should have lost 3 or 4 close games," Weatherbie said. "Our guys found a way to win more close games than they lost that season and that's why we're successful and won a bowl game."

All of it made Weatherbie a hot commodity overnight, and it created an uneasy feeling in Annapolis, where football success had been, at best, fleeting since the Staubach era. A half-dozen coaches had been nothing more than bookends to Welsh's success from 1973 to 1981 with miserable results.

First, Boston College and Kansas came calling. Texas Tech, too. Then Baylor courted Weatherbie. A Baptist school courting a devout Baptist? It was a script seemingly too easy to predict. No one wanted to see the party end, but Lengyel and Navy could do little but wait and hope Weatherbie turned down the advances.

While Baylor remained the most dangerous threat, Boston College was pursuing Weatherbie the hardest, making multiple offers. Kansas and Texas Tech were also in play. "Boston College offered me three times, and had I accepted the offer, I would have been the second-highest paid coach in the country," Weatherbie said. "I was offered by Kansas. Texas Tech didn't formally offer, but they had expressed interest."

Meanwhile, Johnson quietly accepted an offer to become head coach at I-AA Georgia Southern in Statesboro, Georgia, where he had previously been offensive coordinator, between the Army game and the Aloha Bowl.

The pressure to keep Weatherbie, charismatic and extremely well liked at the Academy, was tremendous. "At pep rallies, he would rally the Brigade by pulling his shirt off and swinging it around his head, showing off his barrel-like midsection to the students," said Mike James, then a Midshipman who now blogs about Navy football. "At basketball games, the Midshipmen would chant at Lengyel to extend Weatherbie. And after Army extended Bob Sutton, who was very successful, the pressure only increased."

The prevailing thought was that after finally finding a coach who could put wins on the board, Navy had become a steppingstone to a bigger job and would soon be staring at the same problems it had endured under Tranquill, Uzelac and Chaump. But Weatherbie didn't follow the money to Boston College. He didn't follow his Baptist background to Baylor.

"That was the one job I had thought about several times because of the religious affiliation, the fact I'm Baptist and going to do the things I wanted to do in a Christian environment," Weatherbie said. "But when my wife and I met with them, it wasn't what I thought it would be. I felt like Navy was where we needed to be. My wife and I prayed about it, and I talked to my staff about it, and it was one of those things like we felt we needed to stay right where we were."

For Lengyel's administration, which had already started considering options for a potential replacement, this was joyous news. "After I had taken the [Georgia Southern] job, Navy thought Charlie was leaving to go to Baylor, and they had called me about coming back to take the job," Johnson said. "Of course, he didn't leave."

On December 12, 1996, the *Baltimore Sun* reported that a new contract extension for Weatherbie was in place. Weatherbie would stay, and the collective exhale from Annapolis was palpable and audible. "We've pretty much got it finalized…and we hope it will be signed before the Aloha Bowl game with California," said Jack Lengyel.

The deal extended Weatherbie's original contract into a ten-year agreement, an unbelievable offer not just for Navy but any major college program. It's a contract still recalled and scoffed at around Annapolis. In Lengyel's defense, he did exactly what any other athletic director would have done, especially when Superintendent Charles Larsen was highly motivated to keep Weatherbie and made the resources available to Lengyel to keep him anchored in Annapolis. To no one's surprise, Weatherbie's signature was on the extension's dotted line before the document stopped sliding across the table to him.

The irony is incredible: the rebirth of the program, which started in 2002, could have started in 1997 had two key decisions played out differently: Weatherbie leaves for Baylor or Boston College instead of staying at Navy, and Johnson is in position to claim the vacated seat.

Instead, the flirtation with Baylor and Boston College fell through—news that was met with a huge relief in Annapolis—and a fortuitous "out" of what the Weatherbie era ultimately disintegrated into was missed. "We'll never know because it worked out the way it did," Johnson said. "I had a great run at Georgia Southern. We went 62-10 and won a couple national championships. I'm glad I went back there because I think it prepared me to be the head coach at Navy."

Some recall extending Weatherbie as panic-driven or desperate, but Lengyel couldn't risk letting his coach slip off the hook again. Neither Lengyel nor anyone else could have forecast the disaster on Navy's football horizon.

Weatherbie had won twenty-three of his first thirty-six games at Navy, and in the Aloha Bowl, Navy raced back from a ten-point deficit with two fourth-quarter touchdowns, the last a ten-yard run by backup quarterback Ben Fay with just seconds remaining, to stun California. After the Aloha Bowl, Johnson left, Niumatalolo took his place as offensive coordinator, and expectations soared for 1997. The saying heard most often was "11 in '97," a nod to the fact Navy had many starters, including quarterback Chris McCoy, coming back.

The bravado wasn't false, just unreasonably optimistic that Navy would have an even better season and perhaps even run the table. Predictably, those hopes were crushed almost immediately when the Mids were clobbered, 45–31, in the opener at San Diego State. Wins over Rutgers and SMU righted the ship for a few weeks, but back-to-back losses to Duke and Air Force shook the wind from Navy's sails. They'd finish 7-4, but with two wins over FCS schools VMI and Colgate, Navy couldn't qualify for a bowl without an exception from the NCAA. The Academy applied to the NCAA for the waiver. It was denied.

The 1998 season opened with four losses in five games, including a 49–7 loss to Air Force. Navy finished 3-8, and Weatherbie was starting to expose himself as more of a salesman than architect of a sustainable service academy program. Following the season, Bumpas left for Western Michigan—then a very pedestrian performer in the Mid-American Conference—before reuniting with Patterson at TCU.

On campus that fall, Ryan took over as superintendent, and the misery of the season had his immediate attention. "You go to every game when you're the president or superintendent, and I remember being embarrassed sitting in the stands in Colorado Springs as Air Force pounded us, 49–7," Ryan said. "I didn't think they had better kids; they had a better system.... Like everyone else, I was hoping 1998 was just an aberration. The loss to Air Force was humiliating. My first question was, 'Why are they beating us all the time? They're beating us and Army like a clock.' That was in the back of my mind."

# JERRY MAGUIRE

But what happened to Niumatalolo after the season can only be described as the "Jerry Maguire" moment in Navy football history: Weatherbie asked Niumatalolo to meet him for breakfast at the McDonald's on Ritchie Highway in Arnold, Maryland, and in front of a dining room full of strangers, fired him while looking out at a Safeway grocery store.

Niumatalolo had no idea he was walking into an ambush; he assumed it was to discuss the upcoming 1999 season and recruiting. It's a moment the Academy still winces at. "Those unfortunate situations go down in infamy," Gladchuk said. "The same thing happened up at West Point; they'll never live [it] down."

"Those are mistakes administrators shouldn't make, whether they be head coaches or athletic directors—you treat men that are professionals with dignity," Gladchuk added, "because every coach knows they could get called in and told to move on. You buy into that as coach. It's inherent in your profession. There is no security beyond a contract, and there's no security in a contract. You can still fire anybody at any time."

Gladchuk is referencing the day Army Athletic Director Rick Greenspan fired Bob Sutton on a Philadelphia street corner the day after a 19–9 loss to Navy in 1999, just four years after Sutton earned the Bobby Dodd National Coach of the Year award. It kick-started an inglorious era of football at West Point. Starting with a 1-10 record in 2000, Army would go 47-143 over the next sixteen seasons, including five years of at least ten losses and the first thirteen-loss season in NCAA history.

Publicly, Niumatalolo describes the firing as "deserved" and answers questions regarding the incident with incredible grace. "What he actually said to his wife, Barbara, is anyone's guess," Gladchuk said. Niumatalolo told the *Columbus Dispatch* in 2009 it was a rude awakening for the father of three. "When I got fired, I realized I'm not very talented," he said before Navy's game at Ohio State. "I probably thought I had all the answers. It was probably more a personality difference. I'm kind of a fiery guy. It humbled me and helped me to appreciate things."

College coordinators being dismissed doesn't make for robust news—they often fall unceremoniously when things don't go as planned. Many Annapolitians are shocked today to learn it happened to Niumatalolo almost twenty years ago right under their noses. But the jarring nature of his firing played a big role in Niumatalolo learning to convert the raging passion inside him for the game into a controlled burn. "There's no one [back then] that had a bigger temper than Kenny. He could fly off in a second as a player and as a young coach," Johnson said, laughing. "If you ask Charlie, Kenny's temper is probably why he fired him in a McDonald's. He was probably afraid to fire him in the office. Why else would you do it in a McDonald's?"

Weatherbie regrets it still today. "If I could go back on it, I wouldn't have done it," Weatherbie said. "You never like to fire a coach because when you buy something or put your stamp on something, you're in it for the long haul and make it work."

Weatherbie's salesman-like nature and Niumatalolo's fiery demeanor made for an explosive culture clash. "Charlie was the kind of guy who would come in with suggestions, and sometimes they weren't the greatest, but you had to learn how to handle them," Johnson said. "I had more experience and I'd been a coordinator before, so my response [to Charlie] would be, 'OK. We'll draw up and see how it fits in.' Then he'd leave the room and you'd never see him again and you'd not hear about it again, either."

"When I left and Kenny would hear this, Kenny would tell Charlie, 'That's stupid and we're not going to do this.' You just can't do that. You have to learn how to handle it. You're probably right, but you can't say it. Kenny had to learn how to deal with people and how to channel his passion for the game….Getting fired was probably the incident that made him see it as much as anything."

Niumatalolo landed on his feet as a position coach at UNLV for a three-year stint under the legendary John Robinson, a position Niumatalolo described as a "head coaching apprenticeship." A confluence of events—the coaching carousel, injuries to key performers and the program's eroding identity—was conspiring against Navy football in the late 1990s. Chronic failures dating back to the 1960s hung like an anchor around the neck of the program and invited the inevitable, "They'll never be that good again" commentary, too.

By 1999, most of Weatherbie's original staff had left for other jobs. Johnson, Bumpas, Patterson and Niumatalolo were all gone, and like the movie *Groundhog Day*, Weatherbie was Bill Murray. The misery started repeating itself, week after week. The more Weatherbie and his new staff tried to stop the runaway train, the harder it ran them over. Games started to look, sound and end the same way. Wash. Rinse. Repeat.

Still, Navy posted a 5-7 record in 1999, respectable because six of Navy's seven losses were by seven points or less. Late in a heartbreaking 28–24 loss at Notre Dame, officials gave the Irish an overtly generous fourth-down spot with 1:20 left in the game that allowed Notre Dame to keep possession by mere inches. The game-winning score came forty-four seconds later.

"The second year, 1999, we were 5-7 and should have beaten Air Force in Landover, but we lost," Ryan said. "We did beat Army, but you could see then, Army wasn't our competition for recruits. It was Air Force. We weren't doing badly, but we weren't doing well."

Navy would beat Army, 19–9, infamously costing Sutton his job. Weatherbie didn't know it, but he was next. But it would take some time.

## THE END IS NEAR

The willingness to accept key components of the Air Force blueprint when Weatherbie was hired—there's a deep, abiding dislike for Air Force in Annapolis—sometimes included promises made to recruits that were inconsistent with the Academy's best practices and ethics. Detractors decried the perception that Navy had made moral and ethical concessions against the Academy's deep-rooted principles for football success.

But more worrisome was the talent gap revealing itself between the Midshipmen and their opponents, which needs to be as narrow as possible for Navy to be successful. Brian Madden, a solid signal-caller, couldn't stay healthy, because there wasn't enough talent or depth to protect him. Overcoming a serious injury to a key contributor was next to impossible. Navy would win just six times over Weatherbie's final three seasons, including a 1-10 showing in 2000. The Mids were dragged through the season the way a car drags a broken muffler down the street, losing six games by twenty or more points and surrendering forty points five different times. Navy entered the Army game winless but somehow found a way to win, 30–28.

Ryan was unimpressed.

"We weren't competitive in any game except Army....I had decided halfway through that year we were not getting the kids and we have moved away from the option that Paul [Johnson] had established in 1995 and 1996," Ryan said.

By the spring of 2001, a tsunami of epic proportions was bearing down on the athletic department, and Ryan knew that Weatherbie was, simply put, on borrowed time. "Charlie said he couldn't win with our kind of athletes, and I kept thinking to myself, 'The guy at Air Force, he's in the Hall of Fame, but he's no brilliant guy, and he did it, so Navy can do it.'"

This was the tipping point, and he told Lengyel that it was time to pull the trigger. Lengyel, who had given Weatherbie the ten-year extension and won the Aloha Bowl with him, wasn't on board. "I told Jack, 'We need to do something with our stadium and we're not going to get the money from our alumni unless we turn things around, and Charlie's not the guy to do that. I'm convinced of that,'" Ryan said. "I told him, 'We'll honor his contract. He'll be a wealthy man for the rest of his life, but we need to make a change. We need to put a signal in the ear of Johnson and see if he'll come back.'"

On June 16, Lengyel voted with his feet, announcing that he would retire from the Academy leadership, effective October 1. The decision spurred a lot of speculation about why Lengyel would leave this close to the start of the football season and force a search committee to replace him on such a truncated time table. "The *why* was me saying, 'If you're not going to do this, I need to find someone to help me find the next football coach,'" Ryan said. "It was an awkward time, I admit, but by then, I had figured who we needed to get back: Paul Johnson."

Ryan's comprehensive, internal look at the athletic department—primarily focused on football—had the potential to reshape football at the Academy forever. With the football program in shambles, and unexpectedly forced to hire a new athletic director, Ryan couldn't hire a football coach and an athletic director, so he was forced to play out the 2001 season with Weatherbie. He hired a search firm and formed a committee to approve a new athletic director. The recruiter, Bob Beaudine, was given an arduous task: come up with five qualified candidates and have those names on Ryan's desk in a week. By September, it had come down to two men, one of them being Gladchuk. "I had done some research and saw where he basically got run out of town at Boston College," Ryan said. "It didn't seem like he got a fair shake."

Ryan called Reverend J. Donald Monan, SJ, who was credited with saving Boston College from a fiscal crisis in the 1980s and guiding it into a period of then-unparalleled financial and academic success. "When I asked him about Chet, Don said, 'One of the biggest mistakes I made in my career here at Boston College was letting the press run off a really good man in Chet Gladchuk,'" Ryan said of Monan, who passed at ninety-two in March 2017.

Gladchuk had achieved some phenomenal success at Boston College, including increasing donations for the school's thirty-three sports by 250 percent overall, and 300 percent for women's sports specifically. He'd also overseen the football team earning the highest graduation rate in the nation in three of the last six years he was at BC.

But despite these accomplishments at his alma mater, there had been a gambling scandal within the football program, which made BC officials itchy because it evoked memories of a more serious scandal within the school's basketball program in the late 1970s and early 1980s that would ultimately become the focus of an ESPN documentary called *Playing for the Mob* in 2014.

A highly publicized rebuke by the school's admissions department of two highly ranked basketball recruits preceded the departure of basketball coach Jim O'Brien for Ohio State. So, Gladchuk resigned at BC and landed in Houston, where he had infamously fired football coach Kim Helton for the crime of going 7-4 in 1999.

"I wanted to find out if Chet was serious," Ryan said. "I remember taking Chet into a side room at the airport hotel in Baltimore and saying, 'I think you're the guy for the job, and I think the board feels the same way, but if you agree to take this job, the first thing we're going to do is fire the football coach and find a [new] football coach.'"

That hotel is no longer there—it was torn down and replaced with a parking garage—but Ryan never forgot Gladchuk's answer: "Admiral, I'm your man!"

This was a time when the extraordinary, modern-day success Navy has enjoyed the past fifteen years was unimaginable, and Gladchuk was the unlikely hero who would reshape Navy athletics. His hiring was controversial to detractors of Navy's athletic-minded administration. Those less than enthused by athletics described Gladchuk as a used car salesman who might use Navy as a steppingstone to his next, better job. They had no idea how focused Gladchuk was on taking the first steps toward rebuilding Navy football into a successful, sustainable Division I program.

On the field, 2001 started miserably, just as Ryan knew it would. Before Navy snapped the football in the first possession of the home opener against Georgia Tech, the Mids had to call timeout twice and took a delay of game foul, too. "I remember Bob Rathbun, who was calling the game on television as a neutral play-by-play announcer, saying, 'I knew right there Navy was in big trouble,'" said Navy radio man Bob Socci. Navy suffered the worst loss in program history, a 70–7 defeat, and was embarrassed further when the Yellow Jackets scored a touchdown with thirty-two seconds left.

After the terrorist attacks of 9/11, all college football games, including Navy's September 15 game at Northwestern, were postponed. Gladchuk later canceled the game altogether. "We would have lost that game, too," Gladchuk said.

On October 6, 2001, thirteen days after Gladchuk officially took the wheel as athletic director, Navy hosted the second of three "home" games with Air Force in Washington, D.C. Across the Potomac River, the Pentagon continued to smolder, as victims were still being recovered and identified there and at the World Trade Center in New York City.

Recognizing that the nation was roiling in the aftermath of the most heinous terrorist attack on U.S. soil, the two rivals—who agree on little—would honor the victims by coming onto the field in unison and standing on their respective sidelines at attention for the moment of silence before the national anthem.

Two service academies playing a football game in the wake of a monumental national tragedy? It was eerily similar to the 1963 Army-Navy game in the week following John F. Kennedy's assassination. The nation had changed exponentially, and the Falcons and Midshipmen would respect that principle.

Up in a radio booth, Gladchuk was giving an interview with Navy play-by-play man Bob Socci and color analyst and *Washington Post* writer John Feinstein when Navy came barreling out of the tunnel, head-slapping and high-fiving one another in a manner befitting a game between two rival state colleges. Whatever it was, it didn't follow the plan to recognize the pall of a national tragedy.

Gladchuk was appalled. "We finished the segment and went to break and Chet took the headphones off and was shaking his head," Feinstein recalled. "Obviously, he already knew the program was a dumpster fire. Chet left the booth, and at the first break we had, I turned to Bob and said, 'Charlie won't make it through the end of the season.'"

He was right. The day after a 21–20 loss at Toledo's Glass Bowl, Gladchuk, who had been on the job twenty days, fired Weatherbie with five years left on his contract. Dating back to a 17–6 loss to Temple on September 2, 2000, Navy had lost seventeen of their last eighteen games, capping Weatherbie's Navy record at 30-45. Weatherbie took the news like a gentleman. "He didn't ask any questions, and moved on," Ryan said. "It was a high-road discussion…it wasn't the right job for him."

Almost immediately, rampant speculation about a potential buyout clause dominated radio, television and newspaper reports about Weatherbie's firing. Gladchuk shut down that scuttle, too. "Coach Weatherbie will receive everything he is entitled to," Gladchuk told the *Capital-Gazette* in a statement announcing the firing.

The remaining financial obligation would have been a tough pill to swallow under ordinary circumstances, but Navy was operating at a 30 to 35 percent deficit, much like the deficit Amtrak limped along with for years. Because coaches aren't Department of Defense employees but rather employees of the Naval Academy Athletic Association, salaries have to be funded by profit and donation, and Weatherbie's contract would stay on the books, at least in part, for several years.

All of it was background noise to Gladchuk, determined to break the program's cycle of mediocrity and expand his expectations for the program. Weatherbie was finished. Three weeks were left in a lost season. Making the most of that head start to find the right coach was what mattered.

Thankfully, Ryan rejected the commissioned report's recommendation to roll the football program back into I-AA, but the pressure to get it right was immense. With Weatherbie out, Ryan now had to figure out how to get Johnson back and told Gladchuk of his plan. "Chet Gladchuk is a guy who doesn't swear, and he looked at me and said, 'Who the hell is Paul Johnson?'" Ryan said. "I told him, 'Paul Johnson is a guy who just won two national championships at I-AA and is probably responsible for the success we had in 1996–97.'"

The wrong man had been offered the right extension in 1996. Paul Johnson was in contention for another I-AA title in Statesboro, Georgia. Ryan and Gladchuk had to figure out how to bring him home.

## Chapter 5

# NOTRE DAME

There isn't a school in the country that wouldn't love to have an annual home-and-home game with Notre Dame on its schedule every year. For the last ninety years, only Navy can make that claim.

The relationship the Academy enjoys with Notre Dame has outlasted a lot of brand names and marquee games—notably, Michigan—and the game has been played continuously since 1927. It predates almost every legendary coach or player at either institution. "Division I sports is a big business. Everyone wants to play Notre Dame," Niumatalolo said in the 2015 mini-documentary *Mutual Respect*, aired by NBC Sports. "They could use this opportunity to do other things to help their program, but they've been true to their word as far as this game being important to them."

Of course, it's never been just about the football. This game honors a respectful relationship, forever changed when the U.S. Navy helped the country's foremost Catholic university avoid closure.

Before World War I, both schools were planting the early seeds of their respective programs. In 1887, Notre Dame was defeated by Michigan, 8–0, in its first ever game. Navy met Army for the first time in 1890 and won, 24–0. The paths of Navy and Notre Dame first crossed in the Irish's 19–6 win in Baltimore in 1927. Navy's first win in the series, a 7–0 mark at Baltimore in 1933, was under the direction of Coach Rip Miller, who helped end the Midshipmen's six-game drought.

Miller's arrival at Navy intermeshed neatly with his Notre Dame legacy. Miller was a tackle—part of the Seven Mules and Four Horsemen under

Knute Rockne—on the Irish teams that went 27-2-1 from 1922 to 1924, including the national championship his senior year.

After graduation, Miller was hired by "Navy Bill" Ingram at Indiana for the 1925 season. In 1926, Ingram and Miller transferred their allegiance to Annapolis and led the Midshipmen to the program's only national title, going 9-0-1. Those Midshipmen famously beat Fielding Yost's Michigan team, 10–0, before tying the Cadets in the most revered of all Army-Navy games: the inaugural contest at Chicago's Soldier Field.

But the story most often told—almost ad nauseam—is how the U.S. Navy helped save Notre Dame from a potential closure in the middle of World War II. The Japanese hit the U.S. Navy with a "sledgehammer"[19] on December 7, 1941, dragging America into a war it had been reluctant to join. Overnight, everything in America changed. Private citizens and public corporations alike began rationing. A draft was instituted; no one was exempt, including baseball players. Detroit's Hank Greenberg, Boston's Ted Williams and New York's Joe DiMaggio all traded home whites and pinstripes for military-issue khaki and camouflage.

It changed college football, too. Without students paying tuition bills, colleges close quickly. Many colleges and universities, especially the Land Grant colleges, survived thanks to appropriated funding from state legislatures. But Notre Dame, a private midwestern school that offered an Ivy League–quality education, didn't have the established East Coast power structure to endow it. "During World War II, financially, we didn't have great support," former Irish coach Lou Holtz said. "The Navy, in supporting this program, really kept Notre Dame afloat at that time."[20]

Facing the possible closure, Reverend Hugh O'Donnell at Notre Dame inquired about the U.S. Navy's interest in utilizing the university as a training center. The Navy responded by commissioning a V-12 program in South Bend in July 1943.

The purpose of the V-12 program was to generate a large number of officers for both the U.S. Navy and Marine Corps to meet the demands of World War II, far beyond the number turned out by the United States Naval Academy and the U.S. Naval Reserve Midshipmen's School. Obtaining a commission depended on service branch.[21] The South Bend, Indiana campus was quickly repopulated by 1,851 active seamen, boosting the existing student body of 700.

Ever since the U.S. Navy accepted O'Donnell's plea for help, Notre Dame has been resolute in keeping the game alive. When it aligned with the Atlantic Coast Conference in 2012 to play five games per year, Notre Dame protected three games: Stanford, Southern California and Navy. What has survived and evolved, besides keeping the game on the schedule at each school, is an abiding respect on and off the field between the two schools. Each campus is storied in its own respects and founded on principles and standards eclipsing the importance of any football game or series.

One of the most revered brands in football, college or professional, Notre Dame boasts legendary coaches, Heisman Trophy winners and a fan base expecting to see the Irish compete for a national championship annually. Navy brings a fierce and abiding love of service and country and, since 2003, a triple-option attack that showcases the ability to grind out yardage and clock time simultaneously.

"Playing at South Bend is unlike any other stadium," Niumatalolo said. "I still remember my first game in 1995. I gave a big pep talk to my players. 'Don't get caught up in the hype. It's just another stadium. Their field is just as big as everyone else's field.' And I remember when I first came out, I'm [the one] in awe of this stadium."

Most of the Midshipmen point to this game because many of them grew up watching Notre Dame or came to Annapolis in part because of the opportunity to play in that game. That makes the Notre Dame game a powerful recruiting tool. "Between Army and Notre Dame, those are the two most popular games on the schedule....Everyone in the country are watching those games," former Navy quarterback Will Worth said. "I was a big fan of Notre Dame growing up, so to be able to play and beat them is a dream come true."

For Notre Dame, the challenge is often a battle of will. "You know going into the game that physically, you're going to be able to move them around probably a little better than you are other teams you play," said Tim Brown, a Notre Dame receiver from 1984–87. "But you also know that this is going to be the most disciplined team that you're going to play all year."[22]

That might never have been more evident than in 2016. Navy's 28–27 win over Notre Dame in Jacksonville, Florida, was perhaps the most effective display of the triple-option offense in several years. When executed properly, it wears a defense down and lessens considerably the deficiencies Navy faces in skill and physicality.

The Mids held the ball for twenty-one minutes and forty seconds of the second half, allowing just two Notre Dame possessions, and never officially punted during the game. Navy's Alex Barta did kick the ball away facing a fourth-and-six in the second half. However, during an extended commercial break following the play, it was discovered the on-field officials missed that the Irish had twelve players on the field when Navy snapped the ball in punt formation. A five-yard foul was enforced, and after Navy converted a fourth-and-one, the Mids finished a sixteen-play, nine-minute march that led to Worth's game-winning touchdown. Navy was eight for thirteen on third down and four for five on fourth.

After the game, Notre Dame coach Brian Kelly, while admitting his frustration with the penalty called by replay, said, "They executed flawlessly. It's what we expect every time we play Navy." That win gave Navy twenty-three victories over Power 5 schools since 2003, matching Brigham Young's fourteen-year stretch among the "Group of 5"—Division I schools not playing in the Big Ten, Big 12, PAC 12, ACC and SEC. Next closest is Boise State (fifteen).[23]

The recent success against Notre Dame is another facet of the remarkable change swirling around Navy in the last fifteen years, a stark contrast to the thirty-nine-year stretch from 1964 to 2002 that produced just nine winning seasons. Notre Dame could have justifiably dropped the Midshipmen from its schedule. It didn't. "Some people were saying, 'Get them off the schedule,' and that was not going to happen as long as Father [Theodore] Hesburgh and Father [Edmund P.] Joyce were there," said former Notre Dame coach Ara Parseghian, who came to South Bend in 1964 and was 95-17-4 in eleven seasons. "They had a lot of respect for Navy, and when Navy was down, we didn't kiss 'em off."[24]

## THE STREAK

Nobody could have predicted the unfathomable, NCAA-record forty-three-game losing streak to the Irish back in 1964. The Midshipmen finished 1963 ranked No. 2 by the Associated Press poll and had played Texas in the Cotton Bowl for the national title. Roger Staubach, the Heisman Trophy–winning quarterback, was returning for 1964's Notre Dame game in Philadelphia. "Staubach was a great football player and a dynamic, charismatic human being," said George Goeddeke, who played for Notre Dame against Staubach in 1964. "There was never a game that Navy was out of when he was on the football field."[25]

With Staubach banged up, Navy unceremoniously limped through a dismal 3-6-1 season, and the Irish whitewashed Navy, 40–0, at the newly renamed JFK Stadium. "I didn't have any idea we were going to win it

40–0 because Staubach was there and they had destroyed us the year before," Parseghian said. "But we had some magic with John Huarte and Jack Snow."[26] Huarte won the Heisman. Notre Dame won a national championship. Navy was headed at high speed for the skids.

"The Streak" lasted from 1964 to 2007, spanning the tenure of eight U.S. presidents, ten Navy coaches and eighteen Academy superintendents. It bridged the two most prolific eras in Navy's history: the "Camelot" days of the 1950s and 1960s and the "Return to Glory" renaissance from 2003 to the present day.

Dominated by lopsided losses—just seven of the forty-three games were decided by eight points or less—the Streak included a handful of games close enough to win that felt like a death in the family for Navy fans. There were five fourth-quarter comebacks by the Irish. Twice Notre Dame kicked game-winning field goals on or within seconds of the final play.

By the time Weatherbie took over in 1995, Navy was close to breaking through. From 1997 to 2006, Navy lost four times within the last two minutes. "There was no pressure to keep that streak going when I was here because at that time, we were much superior athletically than Navy was and had been for a very, very long time," said Marc Edwards, a former Irish fullback from 1993 to 1996 who played ten years in the NFL and won a Super Bowl in 2002 with the New England Patriots. "But as a fan, and moving on after I left here, I saw that gap keep closing and closing and closing."[27]

The pressure on Navy to end it was immense, just as it was to keep it going for Notre Dame, too. "I don't want to be the coach that breaks that 43-game winning streak," Holtz said. "I felt greater pressure there than I felt playing Michigan. I know we can't beat Navy every year, but I just don't want it to be *this* year."

Here's a look at the close calls that added life to the Streak, all as memorable as the night the Streak died.

## *1974: Notre Dame 14, Navy 6*

Navy stymied Notre Dame for most of the game, owning the field position battle thanks to John Stufflebeem, who punted eleven times and averaged forty-eight yards per kick, including a sixty-five-yarder. The Midshipmen took a 6–0 lead into the fourth quarter before Pete Demmerle grabbed a six-yard pass from Tom Clements to give the Irish a 7–6 lead.

Forced to pass against the clock and Notre Dame's stingy defense, Navy threw an interception to Randy Harrison, who ran it back forty yards for a score to clinch the win in Philadelphia. The loss was Navy's sixth straight, the final four (Syracuse, Air Force, Pittsburgh and Notre Dame) by eight points or less. Parseghian told reporters after the game, "The way [Navy] played their last four games, they've deserved a better fate."

On the way back to South Bend, Parseghian decided to retire at season's end.[28]

## 1976: Notre Dame 27, Navy 21

At Cleveland's Municipal Stadium, Navy led, 14–3, but allowed the Irish to storm back with three touchdowns in the second quarter to take a 24–14 lead into halftime.

The Irish escaped when defensive back Dave Waymer tipped away a pass at the goal line from Navy quarterback Bob Leszczynski on fourth down with 4:30 left. Navy got the ball back one more time and drove from its twenty to the Irish sixteen, but Leszczynski's pass was intercepted by Luther Bradley in the end zone on the final play.

## 1984: Notre Dame 18, Navy 17

Just how much time was on the play clock? That was the question dominating the post-game of Notre Dame's win in Giants Stadium.

With eighteen seconds left, the Irish's John Carney booted a game-winning, forty-four-yard field goal. Navy contended that the play clock expired before the ball was snapped and that Notre Dame should have been assessed a five-yard foul, pushing the try back to a forty-nine-yard attempt.

Navy coach Gary Tranquill was so certain that he was charging onto the field toward officials to contest Carney's kick as it sailed to the goal posts. "I'd stake my life on it," he said emphatically after Notre Dame had beaten Navy for the twenty-first straight time. The referee, William McDonald, said that the field judge, John Daniels, had lost sight of the clock "for a few seconds because the defense was jumping up and down....In his opinion, the clock did not exceed 25 seconds."[29]

Tranquill was also furious that officials had passed on a foul for roughing the kicker when Navy punter Mark Colby was contacted after kicking the ball back to Notre Dame before its winning score. After the game, he told the *New York Times*, "I don't like to say anything about the officials, but some guys are gutless when the game is on the line."[30]

McDonald told the *Times* there was no foul because "a kicker is no longer a kicker when his foot has returned to the ground," he said. "He was back on the ground when he was hit."

The real culprit, however, was Navy's inability to make six Notre Dame turnovers hurt—including four interceptions thrown by Steve Beuerlein—and allowing Allen Pinkett to run for 169 yards on thirty-seven carries.

## 1997: Notre Dame 21, Navy 17

The frustration continued in South Bend when Navy came tantalizingly close to a miracle finish. Chris McCoy's "Hail Mary" pass on the game's final play deflected off Notre Dame safety Deke Cooper. Pat McGrew, a slotback whose job was to trail the play in search of a deflection, hit the jackpot at the Notre Dame twenty-five. Securing the ball out of midair, McGrew raced for the pylon, but Allen Rossum was faster and knocked McGrew out of bounds at the two-yard line before he could get into the end zone.

"As they threw their 'Hail Mary,' it landed about the 40, and [our secondary] decide they want to get an interception," Rossum said. "The two [defenders] run into each other like a cartoon and the ball comes up in the middle of the air. Lo and behold, the Navy guy [McGrew] is still running… and he catches the ball and takes off running. Luckily, I had a little speed on my side and I caught him and pushed him out at the 1-yard line."[31]

After the game, some of the partisan crowd at Notre Dame Stadium booed Navy for walking through the Irish band while carrying out the customary singing of the "Navy Blue & Gold" and assembling for a prayer at midfield.

"We sing the 'Navy Blue & Gold' and say a prayer at midfield after every game," Weatherbie told the *Baltimore Sun*. "This is the first time we've been booed for praying."[32]

## 1999: Notre Dame 28, Navy 24

Facing a fourth-and-ten from the Navy thirty-seven with 1:20 to play at Notre Dame Stadium, the Irish's Bobby Brown caught a pass and, with two Midshipmen trying to pull him down, earned a first down despite the contentious howls from Navy about the spot being generous. A handful of plays later, quarterback Jarious Jackson eluded Navy's pressure and found Jay Johnson, who made Davede Alexander miss at the five before diving into the end zone. With just thirty-six seconds left, Notre Dame had its thirty-sixth consecutive victory over Navy.

If the spot by officials came up short, the Midshipmen would have taken over, and Notre Dame, without any timeouts, would have been unable to stop the clock. "It breaks your heart," Navy safety Chris Lepore said. "You could call this a devastating loss. A 36-year streak and we came within one centimeter of ending it. It was that close on the fourth down....It was the closest measurement I've ever seen in my life. Call it the luck of the Irish, but it makes this all the tougher to swallow."[33]

## 2002: Notre Dame 30, Navy 23

They were four-touchdown underdogs, but with less than five minutes left, the Midshipmen held a 23–15 lead over the No. 10 Irish. And then heartbreak came back and again punched Navy in the gut.

Navy entered the game 1-8 and lost quarterback Craig Cadet to a sprained left ankle on the game's fourth play. A pair of Notre Dame touchdowns in the final 2:20 lifted the Irish past Navy, 30–23. First, quarterback Carlyle Holiday hit Omar Jenkins with a thirty-nine-yard pass to set up a first-and-goal. Next, Rashon Powers-Neal plowed over the top of the pile to make it 23–21. A wide-open Arnaz Battle caught the two-point conversion to tie the game.

After surrendering one first down on Navy's next possession, the Irish got the ball back at their thirty-three. Holiday found Jenkins on the first play for a sixty-seven-yard strike—a fly pattern on the first play of a possession—to take the lead.

Amazingly, Navy had two more possessions in the final 2:08, but the Irish's Courtney Watson and Glenn Earl intercepted Aaron Polanco, Candeto's replacement, to seal Notre Dame's thirty-ninth consecutive win.

## 2003: Notre Dame 27, Navy 24

For the fourth time in seven years, Notre Dame managed to win despite trailing in the fourth quarter. Down 24–21 with less than ten minutes to go,

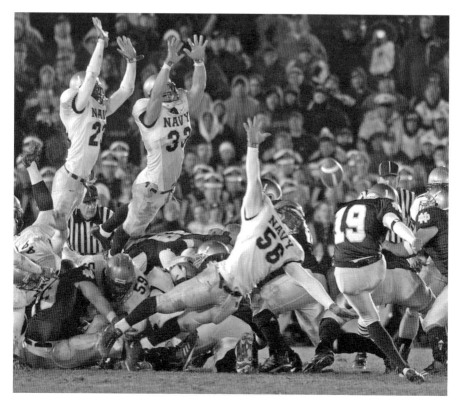

Navy's Vaughn Kelley (23), Josh Smith (33) and Dan Peters (56) try in vain to block the game-winning field goal in 2003 by Notre Dame's D.J. Fitzpatrick. The 27–24 win was Notre Dame's fortieth consecutive win over Navy. *U.S. Navy/Scott Allen.*

Irish kicker D.J. Fitzpatrick booted two field goals, including a forty-yarder on the game's final play. Despite keeping the Irish out of the end zone in the final quarter, Navy couldn't prevent another loss to Notre Dame. "The Navy players fought their hearts out, trying to break that 40 years of frustration," opined Tom Hammond on NBC as cameras panned over Navy's crestfallen sideline.[34]

## *2007: It's Over! Navy 46, Notre Dame 44 (3OT)*

When Navy finally broke through, it did so in epic fashion. In the third overtime, Navy led 46–38, but Notre Dame's Travis Thomas scored a touchdown to make it 46–44. Notre Dame's two-point conversion failed, but a pass-interference flag was thrown against the Midshipmen, a foul Navy coaches and fans still decry as questionable at best.

It mattered not. Navy succeeded in stopping the Irish on the next play, and the Midshipmen jubilantly stormed the field. Tom Hammond, handling the play-by-play for NBC's Notre Dame Network broadcast, was simple yet masterful in his description: "Thomas…fighting…stopped! And this time, it's official! The streak has ended at Notre Dame Stadium on November 3, 2007. For the first time since 1963…Navy has beaten Notre Dame!"

After a few minutes of unbridled celebration, the Midshipmen and the Fighting Irish stood shoulder to shoulder as each school sang their respective alma maters. Navy is the only school Notre Dame employs this level of recognition for. "I just thought that was the coolest thing…ever," Edwards said.[35]

Navy coach Paul Johnson addressed the moment with the media after the game with his typical wit. "It's a big win for our program. It's a big win for the academy," Johnson said in the Associated Press story. "I'm happy I don't have to answer anything else about the streak every time we play."

Later that season, he became just the second coach in Navy history to defeat Air Force, Notre Dame and Army—Navy's three primary rivals—in the same season since Hardin did it in 1960. A week after defeating the Cadets, 38–3, Johnson accepted the head coach's position at Georgia Tech, leaving the wheel for Niumatalolo.

Since that 2007 victory, Navy has defeated Notre Dame three more times—in 2009, 2010 and 2016. With the most recent win, Niumatalolo joined Wayne Hardin as the only coaches in Navy history with three wins over the Irish. Hardin, who passed away on April 12, 2017, remains the only Navy coach to beat Notre Dame three times in four years. Johnson and Niumatalolo split the feat between 2007 and 2010.

Niumatalolo has kept Navy rolling forward the past nine seasons but keeps a large, custom montage of the 2007 victory in South Bend on his office wall. "A big part of that picture shows the jubilation, the years of trying to get over the hump," Niumatalolo said. "Our guys, this is it for them….The NFL dreams pretty much are over after their playing careers, so to have an opportunity to beat a storied program like that was something I'm sure they'll never forget."[36]

## Chapter 6

# JOHNSON RETURNS

## 2002–2007

Chet Gladchuk's interest in coming to Navy didn't include the title of garbage man, but that was his first marching order. But in the late fall of 2001, the football program was rudderless, lacking direction and identity. For Gladchuk, firing Weatherbie was just the beginning.

Five years earlier, the wrong man was given a king's ransom, while the right man for the job quietly walked out the back door. Navy was staring at the potential end of Division I football, and Gladchuk knew the man he needed to hire to fix it.

During Michigan's amazing, thirty-nine-season streak without a losing record from 1969 to 2007, the school's president, athletic director and head football coach were always in lockstep about the importance of the program and how to best execute football's mission.

You don't achieve Michigan's level of success—cementing yourself as a nationally known brand—without that kind of cohesive, layered leadership that was missing from the Naval Academy for decades. Navy would secure a good coach, but the superintendent, commandant or athletic director didn't mesh. Coaches who had been successful—Erdelatz, Hardin and, specifically, Welsh—were forced out or left for other jobs after constant chafing at the Academy's refusal to make changes to promote success as the landscape of college football changed.

No one wanted to see the core values and mission of the Academy change, but there had to be some room to maneuver. Maintain the Academy's traditions? Absolutely, but football had to remain an important vehicle of the Naval Academy's future. Finding a coach or athletic director who was able to articulate the necessary changes and sell it to the military leadership running the show in Annapolis proved difficult.

Gladchuk and Johnson would become the pair to change all that. Internally, support for football was waning after Navy went winless in 2001, and produced just ten winning seasons in thirty-nine years. Outside the walls of the Academy, Department of Defense officials and a growing number of legislators had grown weary of Navy's chronic failures. Calls from politicians and military leaders wanting to wrest control of the athletic department's finances away from the Naval Academy Athletic Association were growing louder.

And it wasn't just the losses. Games became gruesome massacres of thirty points or more. The Midshipmen endured multiple injuries, looked inept and, worse, weren't competitive with their service academy rivals. Support from within the fleet was tough to find, too. "The armed forces network puts television and radio programming out to ships at sea and military bases around the world," said Eric Ruden, now deputy athletic director, of his first few years trying to promote the program. "Back in the mid- and late 1990s, I was always pushing the programming director to carry as many Navy football games as possible. They would always pick up the Army-Navy game, as well as the Air Force game, but I had a very difficult time getting them to carry any other broadcast—on television or radio—because what they perceived to be, and probably rightfully so, as a lack of interest among the soldiers and sailors in Navy football. The feedback I received was there was a stronger connection within the enlisted ranks at that time to their hometown school, whether that be in Oklahoma, Texas, Florida, Notre Dame—you name it.

In military jargon, Navy wasn't just losing the battle; they were losing the war, too. Local and national media believed that the East Coast service academies could no longer regain their foothold from the days of the post–World War II era, and no one wanted to hear the "glory days" stories anymore, either.

Ryan knew this. So did Gladchuk. All they needed was a coach, but this might be the last chance to rebuild the program into a consistent winner at the Division I level. The internal study Ryan commissioned on the athletic program, which focused primarily on how Division I football fit within athletics going forward, recommended Navy drop down to I-AA, now called FCS.

Was winning within major college football no longer feasible at Navy? "The first thing I told Ryan was, 'Admiral, this is the United States Naval Academy. You're NOT going junior varsity with your football program!'" Gladchuk said. "A huge factor in my coming here was Ryan convincing me that we had to get the football program fixed, because there was that looming grey cloud which had to do with Navy going down to I-AA, which I didn't believe. The stadium needs to be fixed, the staffing needs to be fixed. We need renovations. We need energy. We need enthusiasm. We need great leadership out of our coaching staff. Once we fix football, the rest of it will come along."

Wisely, Ryan did not act affirmatively on the report's recommendation, but Navy football was dealing with the same kind of syndrome Ronald Reagan famously labeled the resistance to military involvement in the 1980s. It would be inconceivable to compare Navy football to the end of America's involvement in Vietnam twenty-five years earlier, but there were some interesting parallels to consider. During the early years of America's involvement in Vietnam, the mission was noble, but as more Americans died on the battlefields, the public's tolerance adversely changed. Navy's on-field losses were producing more questions than answers. Worse, financial support for advancing the mission further was being scrutinized by military leaders and policymakers.

In the eyes of many, the fiscally responsible thing for Gladchuk to do would have been to allow Weatherbie to chew down more of the massive, ten-year contract off the Academy's ledger. Navy would have likely continued to lose, because except for an eight-year reprieve under Welsh from 1973 to 1981, that was the most consistent attribute of the program.

The bigger risk is to invest more in hopes of saving the program. College football is an industry, and human capital is what drives the bottom line. When a business is suffering chronic failure, most CEOs don't say, "This is the perfect time to expand the company's vision by spending more."

Gladchuk was undaunted. He knew the program was a front porch to the Academy's larger purpose. Coupled with Ryan's intensity and vision, almost an obsession, producing a winning football program and a winning athletic department was what convinced Gladchuk to take the job.

For the Brigade, attending Navy home games is a military obligation; Ryan and Gladchuk were determined to make it a morale booster and "point-to" event on Saturdays. "Having been at football-dominant schools, and having had the experience of knowing the impact a successful football program can make, I thought it was incumbent on me to educate our Superintendent, our CFO and others in terms of what we needed to do," Gladchuk said. "I'm sure there were some people in the Comptroller's Office and Superintendent's office who were swallowing hard, but I came here to succeed, not to fail, and if we were going down, I was going down with the ship."

Neither Ryan nor Gladchuk was willing to give up the ship, but the football program had become a tumor within the athletic department, when it should have been the strongest muscle. The tolerance or patience to allow it to metastasize further had long passed. If firing Weatherbie was lifesaving surgery, hiring the new coach was the heart transplant.

Rick Lantz was named interim coach for the final three games of 2001, and Navy lost all three, but it mattered little. The victory Ryan and Gladchuk sought was 655 miles away. In the five years since he slipped away, Johnson had won back-to-back I-AA national championships (1999–2000) at Georgia Southern, including five consecutive Southern Conference championships. He was named the Division I-AA National Coach of the Year an incredible four straight years (1997–2000).

While Georgia Southern was preparing for Furman in the I-AA semifinal, Ryan and Gladchuk were preparing to woo Johnson back to Annapolis. It would come down to Johnson and Tim Murphy, the longtime coach from Harvard, but there was no doubt who had Ryan's vote. If Johnson didn't know it already, his name was in the first, second and third slots on Navy's list of candidates.

On Sunday, December 9, Gladchuk joined Tom Lynch; Terry Murray, a retired two-star Marine general who passed in the last week of June 2017; Jim Grant, a former Navy football player serving as Ryan's executive assistant; and Ryan on a passenger military jet at Andrews Air Force Base for this clandestine meeting. Grant and Ryan were in their service dress blues. While trying to arrive in Statesboro, Georgia, the plane had to make two passes—the first to clear the runway of deer. The mission got off to a rocky start almost immediately. "When I agreed to the meeting, I asked them not to arrive in uniforms and Navy apparel," Johnson remembered. "They arrived at the airport in uniform and of course, everyone in Statesboro knew why they were here."

The first meeting was set up at the Hampton Inn on Brampton Avenue, and Johnson let the room know his returning wasn't a slam dunk. "Ryan was telling me how I needed to be in a bigger town, and I stopped him and said, 'I love this place, so we're not going to get anywhere going there,'" Johnson said.

Johnson's comment could have been perceived as bravado or ego—or, worse, disrespect—just as O'Brien's had been perceived six years earlier. Ryan knew otherwise; the confidence from a 62-10 record is real. Johnson was able to turn back all other concerns, too. "We asked him why so few coaches had come from I-AA and had been successful in major college football," Lynch said, "and he was quick to say, 'Yeah? Look at the schools most of those coaches get stuck with.'"

It was exactly the kind of jolt Navy needed. Weatherbie had been confident, too, but he was more salesman, and a salesman's confidence is nothing but a puncher's chance when the losses start piling up. This time, Ryan was talking to the right person.

"People call [Johnson] cocky, but I would call him confident," Ryan said. "Murphy ran a passing offensive, we loved the guy, was smooth and handsome, movie-star handsome, all that kind of stuff, but I kept saying to myself, 'The offense that the Naval Academy needs is the one that keeps the defense off the field,' and that was Johnson."

After the meeting with Johnson, Ryan left marching orders for Gladchuk and Grant: don't come back to Annapolis until you've signed Paul Johnson. It took three days, mostly because there was no cellular or wi-fi service in the Hampton Inn in Statesboro, but the deal was finally hammered out. The challenge became how to pay for what they just bought, especially since Weatherbie would be paid through 2006.

That was the least of Gladchuk's concerns. "In the big picture, that was crumbs—Johnson's salary wasn't a big amount of money—and to get rid of Charlie was lunch money," Gladchuk said. "Paul's salary was big for a guy that works for the government, but it wasn't a lot of money in the world of intercollegiate athletics and what we as an industry were paying football coaches. My guy at Houston made more than [Paul] and the guy at Boston College made three times what Paul Johnson made....As a matter of fact, we mitigated [Charlie's] salary—we never even paid him exactly what his salary was at Navy because he got another job—we only paid him the difference between what he made at Navy and what he made at whatever job he picked up."

The Johnson era began with a very big press conference in Annapolis. He had a track record at the Academy and as a head coach was returning to rebuild the program. Gladchuk had shirts printed for the conference that read, "Expect to Win." Johnson inherited a program in complete distress. Morale was nonexistent, and you needed just two hands to count the number of Division I players on the roster. "We might have had 10

Navy head coach Paul Johnson sends the play in with Lionel Wesley in Navy's 27–12 win over Duke to open 2004. *U.S. Navy/Damon J. Moritz.*

players on the team who could truly play," Johnson said. "We had 220 players on the team but a lot of guys didn't want to play."

What they wanted to do was hang out on the football field, and Johnson wasn't having it. He had the first and second team offense playing against the first team defense, something Weatherbie had shied from out of fear of injury. Suddenly, fullback Kyle Eckel is throwing up on the sideline, and Johnson, who was driving Navy to toughen up, was all over him: "You don't throw up on my time—throw up on your own goddamn time!"

The perks of a hotel room away from the Yard the night before games or avoiding physical training (PT) or marching requirements other Midshipmen endure would now come with a price. The days of hands tucked down the front of their pants and a helmet propped on their head, with just a few players willing to fight for snaps, were over.

"We had to make it mean something to be on the football team, because guys weren't competing," Johnson said. Now Johnson was the garbage man. At spring practice, he filled all eight fields to find out who wanted to compete for playing time. "It was evident almost immediately a lot guys didn't want to be here," Johnson said.

The mantra "Expect to Win" carried past spring practice and into the season opener, a 38–7 spanking of hapless SMU.

But before anyone felt good, the roof caved in. Navy lost the next ten games, surrendering at least thirty points in nine of those games. They lost, 65–19, to North Carolina State; were drubbed by Air Force, 48–7; and were overwhelmed, 46–21, by O'Brien and Boston College.

"In 2002, I'm out begging people for money, selling them on the vision, giving pep talks all over the country promising success," Gladchuk said. "When I would come back home, all I did was try to convince Paul to stay, because after every game he wanted to quit. We went 2-10 and most of the losses were ridiculous."

One loss, a 51–30 shelling at Tulane on October 26, particularly stood out to program insiders. In that game, while it was still close, Johnson had elected to try to convert a fourth down, Tulane had stuffed it and then walked all over the Mids. Following the game, Gladchuk walked the track surrounding the field, completing lap after lap. Later, on the bus, Superintendent Dick Naughton occupied the first seat, simmering in a slow, controlled burn. The contrast between a win and a loss is always remarkable, but this was different. This was raw emotion. Were Naughton and Gladchuk having doubts? Was there concern the option wouldn't succeed? Had they made another bad hiring decision?

The Tulane game left Navy 1-7, and three more losses followed, including a 38–0 drubbing by Connecticut at Navy–Marine Corps Stadium and a 30–23 loss to Notre Dame in Baltimore. A glimmer of light showed itself in that loss to the Irish. Notre Dame rallied for fifteen points in the final 4:30, but despite being twenty-eight-point underdogs, the Mids held a 23–15 lead late in the fourth quarter. Quarterback Craig Candeto had sprained his ankle on the game's fourth play and didn't return, and it still took Carlyle Holiday's sixty-seven-yard touchdown to a wide-open Omar Jenkins with 2:08 left to end Navy's hopes for a monumental upset.

The sun finally came out when the Midshipmen met Army at Giants Stadium and overwhelmed the Cadets, 58–12. Navy scored on their first eight possessions while setting a record for points in an Army-Navy game. Candeto played less than three quarters and still ran for a school-record six touchdowns. "I was on the USS *Nassau* somewhere off the coast of Djibouti, and although I can't remember everyone I was watching the game with, we were ecstatic," said Commander Dave McKinney, who today serves as the Academy's public affairs officer. "It had been so long since we'd seen Navy play that well."

At the banquet, Johnson stood up and said, "In one respect, this was a successful season." Most of the crowd was scratching their heads, looking at one another quizzically. "I did what I was told. At the beginning of the year, Chet told me to 'Expect Two Win.' That's exactly what we had: two wins."

The program was still years away from being able to handle a Power 5–heavy schedule, but in 2002, the Mids played four Atlantic Coast Conference schools, Northwestern from the Big Ten, plus Notre Dame, Air Force and Army. It was a brutal gauntlet for a program in twelve-game recovery, and revamping the schedule into something more manageable was a priority.

Despite being ranked fifth in the nation in rushing, Navy still hadn't turned the corner. The Midshipmen hadn't won at home since November 13, 1999, a 45–21 win over Tulane, which also was the last time Navy had defeated a Division I school not named Army.

The Army game provided a respite, as well as some needed optimism. Another solid recruiting class was in place, a second round of spring practices was under Johnson's belt, and funding for the stadium renovation was marching forward. "I was expecting great things for 2003," Gladchuk said, "and then Hurricane Isabel hit."

A Category 2 storm that made landfall in North Carolina, Isabel roared north and hammered Maryland three days before the September 20 game with Eastern Michigan. Described in the *Washington Post* as a "once in a generation" storm by then Virginia governor Mark Warner, Isabel plowed through Annapolis and Baltimore at high tide, overwhelming the two cities with a record tidal surge.

Downed trees by the thousands dominated Maryland's landscape. Power transformers, exploded during the storm, were ten days to two weeks from repair. President George W. Bush declared a state of emergency for most of the Mid-Atlantic, including the entire state of Maryland.

In Annapolis, downtown businesses rotted in three to four feet of water. Hallways and classrooms at the Naval Academy, which sustained $110 million in damage, were swamped. And the heat that immediately followed the storm was oppressive. Isabel was responsible for forty direct or indirect deaths in D.C., Maryland and Virginia, the city and states where most of Navy's fans come from to attend games.

Gladchuk, staring at as close to a guaranteed Division I win as you could get, was desperate to play the game. "We were so desperate....We had a Division I game, at home, against a school I knew we could beat," Gladchuk said. "We're gonna beat them—that's why I scheduled them!"

But Dave Diles Jr., EMU's athletic director, was wary about sending his team into a federal disaster zone. There was no local hotel to stay at, and it was uncertain if the Eagles could fly into any of the local airports, either. "I had been telling him it would blow over, and he called me and said, 'Chet, I'm looking at pictures of the academy, and it's under water,'" Gladchuk said. "But the stadium was dry, so I talked him into coming. We flew them into BWI [Baltimore-Washington International Airport] and we housed them up in Baltimore, so they didn't really see the devastation."

With the opponent back on board from Ypsilanti—Michigan locals pronounce it "Ip-Sa-Lan-Tee, or "Ip-See" for short—Gladchuk had to save the date at home, too. "Commandant Sam Locklear called me Friday morning and said, 'Chet, we're not playing the game,' I said, 'Dant, we're playing the game,'" Gladchuk said. "What we need is something to cheer about, something to rally about. I know the place is devastated—it's a disaster—but we need to take Saturday afternoon, march over to the stadium and win a football game. Trust me...we can do it."

It didn't take long to accomplish the mission. In front of 27,627, including a weary Brigade of Midshipmen, Navy overwhelmed EMU, 39–7. The Mids forced Eastern quarterback Chinedu Okoro into four first-half interceptions, and the offense rolled up 464 yards, including 421 in the first quarter.

It was Navy's first win over a Division I school not named Army in 1,407 days. "We could not let that game get away, because that was the start of the turnaround we needed," Gladchuk said. "Two weeks later, we beat Air Force and never looked back."

Indeed, Navy stunned the undefeated and No. 25 Falcons, 28–25, at FedEx Field in Washington, D.C. The first win over Air Force in six seasons put Navy in position to win the Commander-in-Chief (CIC) Trophy for the first time in twenty-two seasons and avenged a 48–7 rout from the year before. "They came in undefeated and frankly, after that I don't think they were ever the same," Monken said of the first big win of Navy's revival.

Johnson's trademark wit made its first appearance in the rivalry after the game, as reported by the Associated Press: "After last year's game, they said they wanted to send us a message—got it—back at 'em."

After another big win over Army (34–6), Navy had eight wins and a bowl game to play for the first time since 1996. A 38–14 loss to Texas Tech in the Houston Bowl did little to slow Navy's burgeoning momentum. More important, the culture change Johnson forcefully planted on the field was bearing fruit. "We had whittled [the roster] down and made it special to be on the team again," Johnson said. "At the same time, we put in offensive and

Navy's Josh Smith sacks Air Force's Chance Harridge during 2003's 28–25 upset of the No. 25 Falcons at FedEx Field. *U.S. Navy/ Damon J. Moritz.*

Navy's Kyle Eckel runs over Air Force's Larry Duncan en route to 176 yards rushing and a touchdown in a 28–25 upset of the No. 25 Falcons. *U.S. Navy/Mark D. Faram.*

Kyle Eckel was named Most Valuable Player of the 2003 Army-Navy game, a 34–6 win in Philadelphia. *U.S. Navy/Damon J. Moritz.*

defensive systems so when they watched the tape, they could understand why something was or wasn't working. We weren't asking them to do things they couldn't do."

By the spring practice in 2004, the Academy's rigor was working to Johnson's advantage. Excuses were replaced by personal accountability. "No Excuses. Nobody Cares" became a common refrain inside Ricketts Hall. Military and academic requirements, physical training, homework and company obligations were no longer valid reasons not to perform. "We had to make our players understand they're not the only guys who have to go to class. The guys at the last school who played for me went to class, too," Johnson said. "Everybody has to pass so many hours, practice, condition and lift weights, so stop feeling sorry for yourselves. If anything, feel sorry for the people forced to watch you play."

The seniors on the team—called "Firsties" at the Academy—were leading now, allowing coaches to coach and recruit instead of rebuilding the psyche of the program.

No, they weren't as talented as the most recent Navy teams, but they opened the 2004 season with five straight wins for the first time since 1978. Navy edged Air Force, 24–21; marched over Army, 42–13; and took down New Mexico, 34–19, in the Emerald Bowl in San Francisco, a victory that gave the Mids their first appearance in the AP poll (No. 24) in twenty-five years. The Commander-in-Chief Trophy stayed in Annapolis for a second straight year, and nobody wanted the team to fall back on their watch. "Once we established the culture of being personally accountable, the winning started to happen," Johnson said. "What's funny is we had to build in personal accountability when that's what the Academy is ultimately all about. But in football, we had to instill it."

The ten-win season of 2004 was the first since 1905, and Navy rolled to twenty-seven wins over the next three years. There was a handful of noteworthy victories in those three years—a 37–6 whipping of Stanford stands out the most—but the Mids were beating the schools they should and dominating their service academy rivals. In the five years after Johnson took over, Navy was 9-1 versus Air Force and Army and had produced the first ten-win season in ninety-nine years while splitting four bowl games.

Navy went 8-4 in 2005; beat Air Force, 27–24; and trounced Army, 42–23. The 2006 season ended with a frustrating 25–24 loss to Boston College in the Meineke Car Care Bowl, keeping the Mids (9-4) a point shy of a second ten-win season in three years.

For Johnson, only one more obstacle remained: Notre Dame, along with the nation's longest losing streak against one opponent. Entering the 2007 tilt at South Bend, Navy was an uninspiring 4-4. A 31–20 win over Air Force and a 48–45 double-overtime triumph at Pittsburgh kept up appearances, but in the two weeks leading up to the trip to South Bend, the Midshipmen were demolished at home by Wake Forest (44–24) and I-AA Delaware (59–52), surrendering 103 points in the two games.

Delaware quarterback Joe Flacco, a future Super Bowl MVP, shredded the Mids' secondary, something Johnson admittedly never solved at Navy. "We all know Flacco's pretty good, but we struggled to get stops," Johnson said. "It's easier to play offense than it is to play defense at an academy because it's really hard to find defensive linemen. It's not just the weight requirement at the academy; it's hard for everyone. We can't find them at Georgia Tech. The big, fast, strong guys—guys who can rush the passer, who can affect the play in ways no other player can—are hard to find because there's not enough of them, and they're heavily recruited."

Losing two home games like that isn't a confidence-builder when you're trying to snap a forty-three-game skid on the road and on a national stage. But that's exactly what the Midshipmen did on November 3, 2007.

The Irish were in the midst of an awful 3-9 season and entered the game with just one win, but they owned the mental advantage against Navy. Johnson began chopping down that tree immediately. He told his team they only needed to remember three keys to win the game: "Believe you can win. Believe you can win. Believe you can win."[37]

When the Irish held a 21–14 lead at halftime, he said it again. Navy got the game to overtime by thwarting a fourth-down attempt by the Irish to convert at the Navy twenty-four with forty-five seconds left in regulation.

On the first play of the third overtime, Reggie Campbell hauled in a touchdown pass from Kaipo-Noa Kaheaku-Enhada and then caught the two-point conversion pass to give the Mids a 46–38 lead. Notre Dame's Travis Thomas answered by diving in for a touchdown to make it 46–44, but on the two-point try, Navy's Blake Carter tipped a pass away from Robby Paris. Navy's players and coaches exploded off the sideline. Game over! Streak over!

Except it wasn't. A flag lay in the end zone. Pass interference against Carter. The Navy bench couldn't believe it. Seriously? In their eyes, to even call it questionable was an insult. It was eerily similar to the exaltation Miami felt in the 2003 Fiesta Bowl against Ohio State—that season's BCS title game—when it believed it had halted the Buckeyes to win the national championship. A flag halted that party, and video revealed that the call was a phantom foul. With second life, Ohio State won the game; Miami hasn't been a national title contender since.

Now, Navy's coaches had about thirty seconds to rally their troops back into game mode with the ball on the one-and-a-half-yard line. Johnson surmised that the Irish would run the ball, if for no other reason than because Thomas's touchdown run had been from five yards out. "We told them, 'Sell out on the run,'" Johnson told the *Washington Post*'s Christian Swezey. "We told the corners to sell out. If they pass, they pass. They're not in the end zone yet."

Good call, coach. Notre Dame ran to the right, handing the ball to Thomas. Linebacker Matt Wimsett broke through the line and stood Thomas up at the two. The Mids, sending every hat they could to the ball, swarmed forward and drove Thomas down at the five.

No flags. No second chances. No more broken hearts. The streak was dead.

"If you look at the victories of the first few years under Paul, none of them were on the level of that victory over Notre Dame," said Evan Beard, who played for Navy in 2003 and 2004, graduated in 2006 and represented both Johnson and Niumatalolo as their agent. "That was the big announcement. The Paul Johnson project has worked. A group of Midshipmen proved they could go into Notre Dame Stadium, a legacy program that annually attracts a Top-10 recruiting class, and win. That they've defeated Notre Dame three more times in the last handful of years just backs that up."

Going back to 1963, the youngest player on Notre Dame's roster from that game—the last time Navy beat the Irish—was now at least sixty years old. The current-day Irish could only imagine Navy's pride and relief while they stood, watching the unbridled joy. When the Midshipmen assembled for the alma mater, "Navy Blue & Gold," they were standing mere feet from the ghosts of past failures. The spot where Notre Dame shoved Navy's Pat McGrew out of bounds at the one-yard-line on the last play of the 21–17

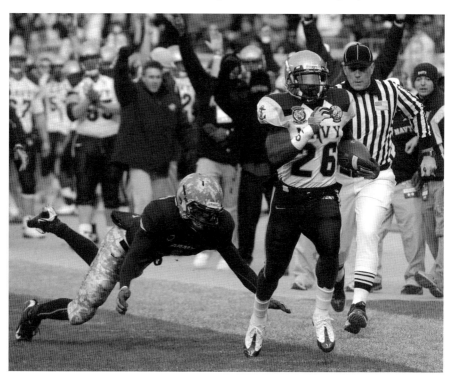

Navy's Shaun White (26) outruns Army's Mario Hill for a touchdown in the 2008 Army-Navy game, won by the Midshipmen, 34–0. *U.S. Navy/Kevin S. O'Brien.*

The Midshipmen and Fighting Irish stand for the playing of "Navy Blue & Gold" after 2007's 46–44 win at Notre Dame, the victory that finally broke Navy's NCAA-record forty-three-game losing streak against Notre Dame. *Jeff Furniss.*

loss in 1997. The goalposts that Notre Dame's D.J. Fitzpatrick had split from forty yards out on the last play of a 27–24 loss in 2003.

Kaheaku-Enhada had led the Midshipmen down the tunnel into Notre Dame Stadium that day, as twenty-one other Navy quarterbacks had during the losing streak, but as Christian Swezey of the *Washington Post* noted, he was the last to leave the field, running back to more than five hundred Midshipmen in the stands to lead a final round of cheers.

Not surprisingly, the win recharged the season for Navy, who outlasted North Texas, 74–62, in the highest-scoring regulation game in NCAA history the next week. "We weren't very good on defense a lot of those years I was there," Johnson said. "The amazing thing about the kids is I don't think I remember an offensive kid say a word about a defensive kid during the years we were there. It was always positive."

After trouncing Army, 38–3, in Baltimore to sweep the Academy's primary rivals—Air Force, Notre Dame and Army—for the first time since 1963, the Midshipmen accepted a bid to play Utah in San Diego in the Poinsettia Bowl.

But Johnson wouldn't be there to see it. On December 7, 2007, Johnson announced that he would be leaving Navy for Georgia Tech. He turned down offers at SMU and Duke. He had accomplished just about every goal a coach could hope to at Navy. He had rebuilt the program, went 11-1 against the service rivals, snapped the Notre Dame streak, groomed a successor and staff and left a blueprint in place to sustain it all. "I informed Chet [Gladchuk] of my decision on a Friday, and before I spoke with him again, he hired Kenny," Johnson said. "The transfer was done before I even came back."

It was done before Navy walked off the field after beating Army, 38–3, in Baltimore. "I kind of tapped him on the shoulder and said, 'Hey Kenny, if anything comes about, I want to talk to you,'" Gladchuk said in an Associated Press article announcing Niumatalolo's promotion.

There was only one question: would Navy continue its upward climb?

## Chapter 7

# "BEAT ARMY!"

There's no game like Army and Navy. Few schools make claim to an iconic football rivalry with worldwide appeal like it. Michigan and Ohio State. Cal and Stanford. Harvard and Yale. More recently, Auburn and Alabama, too.

It's not the "timeless pageantry of brothers in arms" you've seen and heard about hundreds of times before, although that certainly sells tickets and sponsorships. And it hasn't been the yearly importance of the game, either. Since 1930, when the game became annual, the number of Army-Navy games that decided a bowl game or national title number less than a dozen. Often, Army-Navy decides bragging rights and nothing more.

What makes this rivalry special is that more than any other game, it's the nation's game. It's played by a couple hundred student-athletes willing to lay their lives on the line to protect the right for the millions of fans who tune in every year to watch. To be fair, the same principle applies to each academy's game with Air Force, but Army-Navy has been part of American culture for 125 years, and that's the timeless premise fueling the spectacle of service and valor so many Americans adore.

The service academies, by their very nature, harken back to a more romantic era of college football, before a national arms race changed the game into a spending frenzy separating the haves from the have-nots. It's a departure from the nationally known powerhouses, where coaches are hired to be fired and winning trumps all other institutional missions.

The subtle romance to Army-Navy is in the simplicity of a rivalry, both in form and mission. "Beat Navy!" "Beat Army!" This mantra is the rally cry

"Damn the torpedoes—full speed ahead!" Navy kicks off to Army to start the 116th Army-Navy game. The Midshipmen won, 21–17, in Philadelphia. *U.S. Navy/Felicito Rustique Jr.*

behind nearly everything that happens at the Naval Academy Yard, including the weight room, where all the iron plates are impressed with "Beat Army." Monken ends every phone call he takes with, "Beat Navy."

Hall of Fame coaches, Heisman Trophy winners and national title–worthy teams highlight each academy's program, but no matter your pedigree, your success is measured by how well you do in the Army-Navy game.

Upsets and thrilling finishes aside, the game sells out annually up and down the eastern seaboard. It's been around longer than the New York Yankees and Boston Red Sox. By the time the National Hockey League's Original Six teams were fully rooted (1927), Army and Navy had already played thirty times, including the mother of all Army-Navy games, the 21–21 tie at Chicago's Soldier Field in 1926.

The ghosts from the game's glorious past—the 1940s and 1950s for Army and the 1950s and 1960s for Navy—bridge a stretch of years of almost forty years that took its toll on the series. The game's legacy is rock-solid now, having survived the leaner years of the 1960s through the 1990s for both academies.

Today, the game provides an iconic crescendo to the season's end, and that was never truer than in 2016 in Baltimore. Navy entered the game battle-tested but weary, a victim of their own success. For the first time since 1941, the Midshipmen had to face Army without a bye week, and because of qualifying for the American Athletic Conference title game, they were playing their ninth consecutive week.

The Cadets, meanwhile, had three uninterrupted weeks to get healthy and prepare to ruin Navy's season. And while Navy was starting plebe Zach Abey, a third-string quarterback who was believed to be making the first start by a freshman in the Army-Navy game, Army's Ahmad Bradshaw had emerged as a solid signal-caller for the Cadets.

There was a little more than four minutes remaining when the game reached its critical juncture. The Cadets had led, 14–0, after Navy committed three first-half turnovers. Abey's play improved in the second half as Navy roared back to take a 17–14 lead, but Bradshaw's nine-yard touchdown with six minutes left had Army in a 21–17 lead.

Now, facing fourth down and four from his own forty, Navy coach Ken Niumatalolo decided to punt the ball back, betting that his defense would be able to stop Army, get the ball back and drive for the winning score in the waning seconds.

It would be in M&T Stadium's east end zone where one of the two rivals would stage an epic celebration. Either Navy would score to win for the fifteenth time in a row or the Cadets would sing second for the first time in fifteen years.

I walked onto the turf at M&T Bank Stadium with 1:47 to play. Army faced a third down and one from their own forty-five-yard line, and Navy had called their final timeout. If Army picked up just one yard, Navy's streak would end. If the Mids could make a stand, Navy's hopes for a fifteenth straight win would remain alive.

Making what many believed to be the first career start by a freshman in an Army-Navy game, Navy's Zach Abey scores the go-ahead touchdown in the 2016 Army-Navy game, won by Army for the first time since 2001. *U.S. Navy/Felicito Rustique Jr.*

The two teams lined up, and a fog of tension, which had been building to this moment, had the entire stadium paralyzed. Bradshaw took the ensuing snap. The Black Knights' line mashed forward. Navy surged in retaliation, but Bradshaw found his way forward before falling. Officials crashed toward the ball, waving their hands over their heads.

He had gone just six feet, but that was farther than any Army quarterback had gone since 2001. On a meager, two-yard run, Bradshaw ended fourteen years of misery at West Point. "I'm watching the game thinking, 'I cannot believe this is happening,'" Reynolds said. "It was a perfect set of circumstances for them to break the streak. We're down to our third-string quarterback. We had suffered a barrage of injuries. It was a perfect storm and it paid off for them."

Army began kneeling the snap in victory formation as hundreds of jubilant Cadets began bearing down on the railings separating them from the field. After vainly trying to stop them, stadium security finally surrendered in retreat to protect the goal posts. Navy's players, stunned by the loss, looked almost bemused by the show, as if they were finally getting a look at themselves when they celebrated the dozens of upset victories in the last fourteen years. They were. Monken had built the Cadets in the mold of the Midshipmen. "Seeing Army break the streak sucked so bad, I felt like I was playing," Reynolds said. "When I was leaving the game, I felt like I had played and lost. It was a really awkward feeling."

After the final kneel-down, the "Long Grey Line" began advancing forward onto the field, and the black and gold covers began spinning upward into the sky, almost like a graduation celebration. "I honestly just went blank [when] I saw a bunch of cadets running at me," Bradshaw told the *Army News Service*. Edgar Allen Poe, Army's top receiver, was so caught up in the celebration that he lost his head gear: "They took my helmet," Poe said in the same article. "I have no idea where it is."

The singing of Army's alma mater had to be delayed because too many band members had abandoned their instruments in joining their classmates on the field. They had to climb back into the stands to play the Cadets' alma mater.

Those fifteen minutes reinforced how remarkable the last fifteen years in Annapolis had been. Beating the Midshipmen had become this epic for Army, which had struggled with both brand and relevance while Navy reached heights no one thought imaginable when Paul Johnson was hired as head coach on December 8, 2001. A dozen bowl games and a handful of national rankings have thrilled Navy's large national following, helping Navy evolve from primary rival to Army's "evil empire"—like the Yankees are to the Red Sox—and the benchmark for the Cadets to strive for.

In this respect, Army's win in Baltimore was uniquely like Navy's 46–44 win at Notre Dame in 2007. Following the victory, hundreds of Cadets took pictures on the field and in the stands with the final score burning in the background, a moment only imagined until that night in Baltimore. In defeat, Navy's success and swagger built over fifteen seasons was part of the victorious mystique for Army's faithful.

## THE STREAK

In a series formerly punctuated by how closely contested the overall results were over the years, Navy's fourteen-year winning streak was remarkable because no win streak on either side had previously eclipsed five games.

Many of the Army games from 2002 to 2015 were decidedly lopsided. In Navy's fourteen wins, the Midshipmen averaged thirty-one points, the average margin of victory being nineteen points. The Mids reached thirty

Adam Ballard (22) rolls past Cason Shrode (54) and Taylor Justice (42) for one of two touchdowns in the 2005 Army-Navy game, a 42–23 win. *U.S. Navy/Johnny Bivera.*

or more five times, forty-plus points twice and hung fifty-eight on the stunned Cadets in 2002. The only thing tamping down Navy's dominance was a handful of closer-than-expected games where Army stayed within a touchdown of the Midshipmen.

On the other side, Army averaged just twelve points per game in those fourteen losses, scoring less than ten on six different occasions. From 2007 to 2009, the Cadets scored just two field goals in three games. In 2003, Army suffered the indignation of becoming the first FBS team to go 0-13.

Still, Army pushed Navy to the doorstep of defeat a few times, but that's what separated the accomplished Midshipmen from the hopeful Cadets—the ability to finish. "We had been so dominant in the game, and no matter what kind of success Army had, they didn't know how to beat us," Reynolds said. The highlights of the streak include the following games.

## *2002: Navy 58, Army 12*

Navy opened 2002 with a convincing win at SMU, followed by ten consecutive losses—many of which were blowouts—before stomping on Army like a Jeep drives over jellyfish. Quarterback Craig Candeto had the game of his life, rushing for six touchdowns and throwing for another, while the Mids annihilated the series' single game team records.

The forty-six-point margin was the most since 1973's 51–0 whitewash of Army in George Welsh's first year, and the fifty-eight points were the most in the game's history. Navy's 421 yards and 508 total yards also set new single game marks.

It was the third win over the Cadets in four years, so beating Army wasn't foreign in Annapolis, but the manner of the victory certainly was and it would kick-start something no one thought imaginable.

## *2009: Navy 17, Army 3*

The dichotomy of the two programs was never more evident than after Navy's eighth-straight win in the series.

A bowl berth awaited Army in Washington, D.C.'s EagleBank Bowl if they could break the streak, and they led, 3–0, at halftime. But Ricky Dobbs took over as Navy rattled off twenty-three scrimmage plays in the third quarter to just four for Army. A play-fake by Dobbs left Marcus

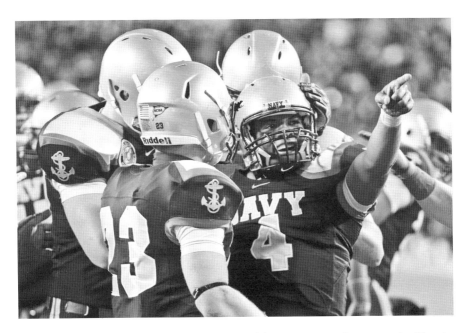

In the 2009 Army-Navy game, Ricky Dobbs (4) celebrates a one-yard score, putting Navy in front and setting the NCAA record for most touchdowns in a season by a quarterback, later broken by Keenan Reynolds. Navy won the game, 17–3. *U.S. Navy/Chad J. McNeeley*.

Curry alone in the end zone, and Dobbs found him from 25 yards out to grab the lead. A field goal made it 10–3, and after fullback Kingsley Ehie botched the handoff from quarterback Trent Steelman, Navy's Craig Schaefer recovered and ran the ball back down to the twelve. Dobbs, who managed 113 yards rushing and passed for a touchdown, scored from a yard out to seal Army's fate. Rich Ellerson, like eight Army coaches before him, lost his first game against Navy.

Navy now owned the service academy platform, with eight wins in a row over Army and seven straight over Air Force. They were an incredible 15 for 15 in service academy games dating back to the 58–12 win in 2002. The Mids went on to pound Missouri, 35–13, in the Texas Bowl and finished 10-4, just the third season of ten wins dating back to 1905.

## *2012: Navy 17, Army 13*

Army was on the doorstep of victory. The Cadets had led, 13–10, and it could have been 16–10, but Eric Osteen missed a thirty-seven-yard field goal with 6:57 left. Reynolds, the first freshman to start at Navy since 1991, made that mistake look bigger when he put the Mids up with an eight-yard touchdown with 4:41 to play.

With 1:04 to play, Army had the ball on the Navy fourteen, and the Mids' defense was gassed. The hands were on the knees for the Mids' interior defenders after every play. All Steelman had to do was push Army into the end zone, and the Cadets would snap the streak, which stood at ten games. "Were we beat? Yeah…," Niumatalolo said.

Steelman took the next snap and pivoted to hand the football to Larry Dixon. The ball skidded away from Steelman before he could shove it into Dixon's belly. Navy's Barry Dabney fell on the ball a half second before Steelman, whose lament was captured by Feinstein. "I feel like we should

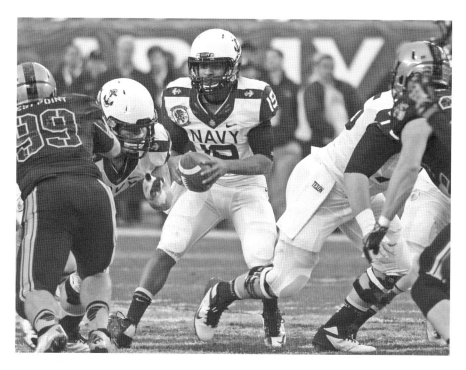

Keenan Reynolds, then a freshman, dodges past Army during the first of his four wins over Army. The pride of Antioch, Tennessee, Reynolds became the first Navy quarterback to go 4-0 versus the Cadets. *U.S. Navy/Chad Runge.*

have won," Steelman said softly, his eye black staining his face because of the tears he had shed in the final seconds. "I thought we deserved that game in every possible way."[38]

Television cameras, over and over, documented Steelman's despair, who said goodbye to the rivalry in inconsolable agony. This wasn't just the most disappointing loss during the streak, and it wasn't just football... it was Shakespearean heartbreak. "There's talk about this [last] year and some of the stuff that happened for Army to break the streak, but Ellerson had us a few times. He just couldn't finish," Niumatalolo said. "Now the talk is about with [Jeff] Monken they've turned the corner and they're coming around and they've closed the gap...but a lot of those games [during the streak] were close games."

## *2013: Navy 34, Army 7*

As sleet and snow blanketed Philadelphia, the Mids snowballed the Cadets, kick-started when the Mids' C.J. Johnson fortuitously fell on a fumble by Army quarterback A.J. Schurr. Noah Copeland and Keenan Reynolds scored touchdowns to put Navy up, 17–0, at the half.

Neither snow, sleet, rain or Army will stop Keenan Reynolds from delivering a 34–7 win over the Cadets in the 2013 Army-Navy game. *U.S. Navy/Marvin Lynchard.*

Reynolds would add two more scores, the last with just forty-six seconds left and Navy on Army's one. Niumatalolo elected to let Reynolds run the ball instead of taking a knee, and his quarterback's final touchdown gave him 176 points on the season, breaking a ninety-six-year-old school record held by "Navy" Bill Ingram (174). Reynolds's effort also set NCAA's single-season record for touchdowns by a quarterback, breaking the shared record of twenty-seven by Ricky Dobbs (2009) and Kansas State's Collin Klein (2011).

"The thought did come across my mind to take a knee," Niumatalolo said in an Associated Press report. "But then my thoughts went to, I have a kid that has a chance to break a record that's hard to come by."

## 2015: No. 21 Navy 21, Army 17

The Cadets were in position to ruin Keenan Reynolds's attempt to become the first Navy quarterback to go 4-0 against Army, but three turnovers in the final quarter and a missed field goal doomed Army.

The Black Knights led 10–7 to end the first quarter, but Reynolds, who entered the game as the nation's top rushing quarterback, scored to push Navy back in front. Just before half, Poe scored from twelve yards out, and Army had the lead at half, 17–14. After Navy stuffed Army's first possession of the second half, Navy took the ball at midfield, and Reynolds found Jamir Tillman with a fifty-yard missile—Tillman still had to dive across the goal line to score. Navy regained the lead, 21–17.

Navy quarterback Keenan Reynolds (19) marches toward the end zone in the Mids' 21–17 win over Army, the record fourteenth straight win in the rivalry for Navy. *U.S. Navy/Damon J. Moritz.*

Army committed one miscue after another the rest of the way. A missed twenty-nine-yard field goal early in the fourth quarter preceded Army quarterback Chris Carter's fumble, recovered at the Navy thirty-four by Ted Colburn. Later, Carter's long pass was picked off by safety Lorentez Barbour, and as time waned, an ill-advised option pass by Army's Andre Bell was intercepted. Incredibly, Army had a final chance still, but a Hail Mary on the game's final play fell short.

Moving to 8-0 versus Army, Niumatalolo tied Army legend Earl "Red" Blaik, who went 8-8-2 against the Midshipmen, for most wins in the series.


## "UNCLE"

In any great rivalry, there is a point-to "Uncle" moment. For Navy, there's two such moments: the hiring of Eddie Erdelatz in 1950 to combat the meteoric rise of Army coach Earl Blaik, and the hiring of Charlie Weatherbie in 1995 to build a program like that of Air Force's Fisher DeBerry.

Army's "Uncle" moment was the hiring of Monken in December 2013. A Navy assistant who coached slotbacks and was the special teams coordinator from 2002 to 2007, Monken watched as many Army games became glorified Navy highlight films. He would become the sixth coach charged with ending the streak.

Like Niumatalolo, Monken had followed branches of the tree planted by Paul Johnson. He followed Johnson to Georgia Southern from 1997 to 2001, at Navy from 2002 to 2007 and, finally, Georgia Tech in 2008. He further followed his mentor's footsteps as head coach at Georgia Southern from 2010 to 2013.

Monken's appointment on December 24, 2013, was an admission from West Point that its archrival had so far surpassed their program that the need was to replicate it, not rebel against it.

The 2016 win over Navy was easily the biggest Army win in at least ten years, if not more. After two lackluster seasons, the Black Knights joined Air Force and Navy and posted a winning season in 2016, the first time all three academies had done so in the same season since 1996.

Suddenly, the Cadets were rock stars. The image of thousands of them swarming the field was college football's final snapshot of the regular season. Hundreds of Cadets took pictures with the lights burning the final score in the background, similar to Navy fans in 2007 after breaking the forty-three-

Noah Copeland runs past the sleet, snow and Army's best efforts to tackle him for Navy's first touchdown of the 2013 Army-Navy game, a 34–7 Navy win. *U.S. Navy/EJ Hersom.*

game losing streak at Notre Dame. "I was on the front end of that Navy streak when it started in 2002. It was a great source of pride to go 6-0 against Army and 5-1 against Air Force, and 11-1 in academy games under Paul Johnson," Monken said. "It's a great feeling, for our kids especially, for our university, for the Army."

The afterglow didn't last long. A week later, Army was outed for its involvement in the "WakeyLeaks" scandal. Tommy Elrod, Wake Forest's former assistant coach turned radio broadcaster, was embittered when he wasn't retained on staff by Coach Dave Clawson, who was named head coach in December 2013. As retribution, Elrod was soliciting proprietary information from Wake Forest's game plans to opposing coaches. The breach was first discovered on November 12, 2016, when documents from Wake Forest's game plan were found in Louisville's locker room after the Cardinals' 44–12 win. Virginia Tech was also implicated, and while Louisville's involvement surprised no one—the Cardinals' athletic department has spent the last two years apologizing consistently on behalf of Coaches Rick Pitino and Bobby Petrino—Army's involvement was a massive disappointment.

With the Cadets' 21–13 win October 29 over Wake Forest clouded, Army Athletic Director Boo Corrigan issued a statement: "Given the seriousness of these claims, it is important that all the facts and findings are gathered and analyzed to determine what action, if any, is warranted."

In no hurry to keep a story of a potential honor code violation in the national news cycle, Army answered media requests by saying an open investigation by an appointed U.S. Army officer had been initiated. To those entrenched within military football, the question of possible separation of an Army coach was omnipresent, especially because the optics at first glance looked bad. After losing in 2014 and 2015, Elrod's betrayal preceded Army's win.

On February 7, Jay Bateman, Army's defensive coordinator, was suspended two weeks and fined $25,000. Army's investigation concluded that Bateman took information from former Army assistant coach Ray McCartney, who left in 2015, and passed it to Bateman. The Army report also said the NCAA did not consider the breach a violation because it fell outside of its jurisdiction. The Academy said it was using the forfeited

After Army defeated Navy in 2016 for the first time in fourteen seasons, the wild celebration for Coach Jeff Monken (*center*) and his Black Knights included approximately two thousand Cadets storming the field in Baltimore. The win revealed how Navy had become Army's "evil empire." *USMA Sports Information/Danny Wild.*

salary toward ethics training. "Our commitment is to foster a culture of excellence and winning in everything we do," Superintendent Lieutenant General Robert L. Caslen Jr. said in a statement. "It does not mean that we win at all costs."

Monken, a Navy assistant from 2002 to 2007, addressed the scandal directly. "They [Wake Forest] had someone in their camp that was giving information out, and we as a program, didn't discern more discreetly and carefully what information should we take and where's the line on this?" Monken said. "As coaches, as strategists, we want to gather information wherever we can get it. When information comes our way, sometimes, we're a little caught off guard. You want to help your team. There's a bunch of guys counting on you and you want to do the best you can and help the team….Someone offers you information, and it's there, and it's difficult to say, 'No, I don't want that information.'"

Monken's point is fair. Coaches ask their peers about formations, special teams situations and audibles every week before film is exchanged between opposing schools and game officials. "Did it really help us? No…but it doesn't change the fact there was information being talked about and information was exchanged."

Monken and Clawson were on staff together at Buffalo while Clawson and Bateman worked together at Richmond. Did the scandal affect those friendships? "I hope not.…I'm sure initially he had some hard feelings, because you're hurt…you've been sabotaged," Monken said. "I think a lot of the hurt is there was someone on the inside that betrayed a level of trust."

## ALL IN GOOD FUN

The proximity along the eastern seaboard and the similarity of the two East Coast academies is what delivers an equal amount of angst and respect between the two rivals. Among the hundreds of anecdotes, stories and history surrounding the game, these are some of the best.

All great rivalries include a healthy number of stunts surrounding the game. My favorite prank, above all others, took place in 1971, when a story circulated that President Richard Nixon would attend the game. Inside John F. Kennedy Stadium, a limousine drove past the Cadets, who stood at attention and saluted the commander in chief. When the vehicle came around and stopped in front of the Midshipmen, the door opened and out stepped…a goat. Navy had the best laugh, but Army got the last laugh—the Cadets won the game, 24–23.

## PRESIDENTIAL PARDON

The game has, for more than one hundred years, invoked such intense feelings that it was famously—or infamously—nearly settled by a duel by an Army brigadier general and Navy rear admiral in 1893, when Navy beat Army, 6–4.

Following the Mids' 6–4 win over Army in 1893 at Thompson Stadium—since demolished but then located on the current site of Lejeune Hall—a duel between a brigadier general and rear admiral following the game nearly marred the day.

A handful of fistfights dominated the action in the stands, too, and this—plus the near altercation between the respective brasses of the two branches—got the attention of Grover Cleveland. The president assembled a cabinet in February 1894 to discuss the game's future. The result? The two rivals could not meet indefinitely. It took an impassioned letter in 1897 from Theodore Roosevelt, then assistant secretary of the navy, to Secretary of War Russell A. Alger:

*My dear General Alger,*

*For what I am about to write you I think I should have the backing of my fellow-Harvard man, your son. I should like very much to revive the football games between Annapolis and West Point.*

*I think the Superintendent of Annapolis, and I dare say Colonel Ernst, the Superintendent of West Point, will feel a little shaky because undoubtedly formerly the academic routine was cast to the winds when it came to these matches, and a good deal of disorganization followed.*

*But it seems to me that if we would let Colonel Ernst and Captain Cooper come to an agreement that the match should be played just as either eleven plays outside teams; that no cadet should be permitted to enter or join the training table if he was unsatisfactory in any study or conduct, and should be removed if during the season he becomes unsatisfactory; if they were marked without regard to their places on the team; if no drills, exercises or recitations were omitted to give opportunities for football practice; and if the authorities of both institutions agreed to take measures to prevent any excesses such as betting and the like, and to prevent any manifestations of an improper character—if as I say all this were done—and it certainly could be done without difficulty—then I don't see why it would not be a good thing to have a game this year.*

*If you think favorably of the idea, will you be willing to write Colonel Ernst about it?*

THEODORE ROOSEVELT

President William McKinley acquiesced, and Army's 17–5 victory restarted the series in 1899. Two years later, after McKinley was assassinated, Roosevelt was president and started the tradition of American presidents sitting on each team's side during the Army's 11–5 win over Navy.

As an aside to his obvious contributions to the Army-Navy game, it was Roosevelt who, following a season that included nineteen deaths in the college game, called the presidents of Army, Navy, Harvard, Princeton and Yale to the White House. This group formed the Intercollegiate Athletic Association of the United States, which later became the NCAA.

The tradition of sitting on one team's side for the first half and switching to the other half was highlighted in a telegram John F. Kennedy sent to coach Wayne Hardin just days before the 1963 game. Kennedy was a Navy man and penned to Hardin, "I hope to be on the winning side when the game ends," in a telegram dated November 20.

Of course, Kennedy was assassinated in Dallas three days later, and the game became an anchor for the country's healing, much like the 2001 World Series between the Yankees and Arizona Diamondbacks was in the aftermath of the September 11 terrorist attacks that year.

There are dozens of books, new and old, and hundreds of newspaper and magazine articles romancing the game, and many of these works populate the pageantry of the game. The draw of a game played by a few hundred players willing to die to protect the lives of a sellout crowd and the millions watching them play on television is a huge part of the game's draw annually.

Over almost 120 years of the rivalry, the game has often been about bragging rights and little more, sans a handful of games where a perfect season or a stake in the national title was in the balance. The annual bit of military theater, greater than any other game, makes the Army-Navy legacy a little sweeter.

The nation's game.

# Chapter 8

# A BALL OF FIRE

## 2008–PRESENT

If Ken Niumatalolo is your neighbor, you think he's a great guy. But if you play football for Navy, in an instant, he can be your worst nightmare. "People see me outside of the field [and] think I'm a nice guy, but I'm a prick," Niumatalolo told me in February while gazing onto the picturesque Spa Creek Inlet from a full-length window in his office in Ricketts Hall. "I hate to lose. You've got to be competitive in this profession or you're in the wrong job."

From his office in Ricketts Hall, which boasts the best view of the Annapolis harbor as any office at the Academy, there's a fire that burns inside Niumatalolo, now the Academy's winningest coach. During the last twenty-two years, Niumatalolo—the first Polynesian coach in Division I history—has been part of twenty of those seasons. He spent four years (1995–98) under Weatherbie, six more under Johnson (2002–7) and, counting 2017, the last ten years as head coach.

A bevy of helmets produced exclusively for Army-Navy games of the past ten years lines the tall credenza of Niumatalolo's desk. A dozen baseball-sized bowl game rings sit neatly on the desk's front edge. Pictures of Navy's biggest games—and pictures of him and his team celebrating the Commander-in-Chief (CIC) Trophy in the Rose Garden of the White House, most recently with President Barack Obama—dot the walls.

But when you ask Niumatalolo about all of it, if it happened yesterday, it might as well have happened at Gettysburg. "We had a great season in 2016, but I don't want our guys looking back because [it's] irrelevant,"

Secretary of the Navy Ray Mabus shakes hands with Navy football coach Ken Niumatalolo before the 2014 season opener in Baltimore against Ohio State University. *U.S. Navy/Nathan A. Wilkes.*

Niumatalolo said. "People know who we are, and that's why it's harder and harder to win games."

Overt reminders of unfinished business from 2016 hang in his staff's war room: Air Force holding the CIC Trophy, Temple celebrating the AAC championship on Navy's field and Army celebrating the first win over the Mids in fifteen years.

Navy moved forward with Niumatalolo late in 2007, right after Paul Johnson left for Georgia Tech. From 2003 to 2007, Navy led the nation in rushing in four of five seasons—including the last three—which had never happened before in NCAA history. The Mids were averaging a school-record 352 rushing yards per game when Niumatalolo took over. That Navy lost his first game, the Poinsettia Bowl, 35–32, against Utah, mattered little.

Gauging potential long-term success on a bowl game is dangerous because schools are paired in these games for two reasons: either it's part of an already negotiated conference tie-in or organizers think it will quickly generate ticket sales. Michigan State made that mistake after Nick Saban left East Lansing for LSU at the end of the 1999 season. MSU Athletic Director Clarence Underwood tabbed running backs coach Bobby Williams as interim coach. MSU defeated Florida, 37–34, on Paul Edinger's thirty-nine-yard field goal as time expired in the Citrus Bowl on January 1, 2000. Recognizing that all of Saban's assistant coaches rebuffed his invitation to join him at LSU, including

Mark Dantonio, Underwood handed Williams the reins soon thereafter. Midway through the 2002 season, after losing at Michigan, 49–3, Williams was fired. Including the bowl game, the Spartans were 16-17 and had lost four consecutive games when Williams was dismissed.

Asked in the post-game press conference by FOX Sports Detroit's Mickey York if he had lost control of the team, Williams replied, "I don't know." MSU Athletic Director Ron Mason fired Williams the next day. It would take two more coaches and more than ten years for the Spartans to return to prominence.

Judging Williams on the strength of a single game was a mistake, just as it would have been wrong to conclude on Niumatalolo in the same fashion. But after winning the 2008 season opener, the Mids dropped back-to-back games to Ball State and Duke. Niumatalolo's first four games were losses to three pedestrian Division I schools and a win over Towson, then a cupcake that would later rise to play in the 2013 FCS title game. The Midshipmen rallied to win seven of their last ten games, including a twenty-seven-point rally—the largest fourth-quarter comeback in school history—to beat Temple in overtime, 33–27, and a 34–0 whitewash of Army.

President George W. Bush congratulates Navy football coach Ken Niumatalolo after presenting the Commander-in-Chief trophy at a White House Rose Garden ceremony, April 14, 2008. *Department of Defense/Chad J. McNeeley.*

In the EagleBank Bowl at RFK Stadium in Washington, D.C., Wake Forest beat Navy, 29–19, but there was no doubt the momentum of the previous six seasons was going to continue. Opening 2009 at Ohio State as twenty-one-point underdogs, Navy came tantalizingly close to upsetting the No. 6 Buckeyes. Niumatalolo's ability to rally his troops was on display for 105,092 people—then the largest crowd to see an OSU opener at Ohio Stadium—and a national television audience.

The Midshipmen trailed 29–14 but rallied for two touchdowns in four minutes to draw within 29–27 with 2:23 left. But on the two-point try, Brian Rolle stepped in front of Ricky Dobbs's pass over the middle and ran it back ninety-nine yards for a two-point defensive conversion. "We played in an All-Star game together after the season, and [Rolle] joked about that play," Dobbs said. "As much as I'd love to have that play back, it is what it is. We made a great comeback, but he made a great play and read on it. That's what competition is at that level."

After the game, most of the media discussion centered on what Ohio State had to do to improve in advance of a showdown the following week with Southern Cal, instead of what Navy had done to disrupt and nearly upset the more talented, highly regarded Buckeyes. The Mids still had a long way to go to earn respect from college football's national media. After the game, Niumatalolo told the Associated Press, "If Ohio State comes in totally focused on us, we had no chance. We felt like we had them in the perfect storm."

Publicly, this is part of Niumatalolo's genius. He plays the "I'm just a second banana" stuff beautifully. Privately, Niumatalolo stokes the fire inside his team as well as anyone. In practice, off-season workouts and spring ball, he drives his team to strive for and expect more precision than any other team in the country.

In this respect, Niumatalolo emerges as the perfect captain of an underdog ship. He and his staff knew who to recruit and how to do it. How to motivate each day, each game and each season. And whenever a big-name opponent or a power conference school is in front of the Mids, he reminds his team how few of them had been recruited by the school or whatever conference is being represented by Navy's opponent.

After losing to Ohio State, the Midshipmen won ten of thirteen, sweeping rivals Air Force, Notre Dame and Army for the second time in four years and just the third time in school history. After winning the CIC Trophy with a 17–3 victory over Army, they trounced Missouri, 35–13, in the Texas Bowl.

Dobbs dominated that game, running thirty times for 166 yards and three touchdowns and threw for 130 yards and a touchdown, too. The media focused on how Navy held the ball for almost forty-one minutes. Dobbs joined Craig Candeto as the only Mid to run and pass for 1,000 yards in a season.

But in the Tigers' locker room, Missouri's Sean Weatherspoon, a future NFL linebacker, shed light on the unique frustration that accompanies trying to defend Navy's triple-option offense. "We knew what they were going to do," Weatherspoon told the Associated Press, "but the thing is, they kind of take your instincts away from you." A change in perception was afoot. Navy's 10-4 record was just the third ten-win season since 1905, but the second in six years.

His players call him "Coach Niumat"—pronounced "nee-ah-mot"—but to call Niumatalolo anything but a competitor would be a big mistake. That was never more apparent than in Navy's 2010 season opener with Maryland in Baltimore's M&T Stadium, a game where his famed temper returned for an instant. But he had good reason to be mad: Navy gave away a 17–14 loss to the Terrapins, a team that lost seven straight games to complete a 2-10 season in 2009. The Mids racked up 485 yards (to just 272 for the Terps) but was denied victory on the game's last play when Dobbs was stuffed at the goal line by Kenny Tate.

It was all part of a bigger frustration. Navy had gone inside the Terps' red zone seven times and managed just two scores, including going 0-for-4 inside the five. Dobbs fumbled twice, and Niumatalolo still elected to go for it on the game's final play.

Worse, an angry outburst between Niumatalolo and Atlantic Coast Conference referee Brad Allen just inside the tunnel at Baltimore's M&T Bank Stadium at halftime was caught on national television. Niumatalolo thought Maryland's players were slow to get off the ball and the pile near the goal line near the end of the half. Replays of the argument, and not of the plays Niumatalolo was questioning, circulated on ESPN for two days.

Alpha male personalities make up the lifeblood of major college football, so coaches, players and officials disagreeing is hardly news. It's not the first time an official and coach have had a heated exchange, either.

Niumatalolo's dust-up with Allen looked worse than it really was. The two made amends before the second half started, and neither man received any corrective action. This wasn't the combative assistant from fifteen years earlier, but the coach's pilot light could still explode. Navy had clearly pivoted from a program that only made headlines when it won a game it

Ricky Dobbs runs during Navy's 14–6 loss at Air Force in 2010. *U.S. Navy/Chad J. McNeeley.*

wasn't supposed to win to a program that made news when it lost a game it shouldn't, too.

The national headline was "Maryland Stuns Navy," a huge change from years past. As Niumatalolo told the Associated Press, "I can't remember a time we rushed for 400 yards and lost."

The Midshipmen rallied to win five of the next six, including the impressive 35–17 beatdown of Notre Dame in the Meadowlands. The only loss was a bitter 14–6 setback at Air Force, and at 9-4, another solid season was in the books. However, bigger decisions loomed.

## TO JOIN OR NOT TO JOIN

The renaissance of Navy football, dating back to 2003, was approaching a decade. The Midshipmen owned their service academy rivals, beating Army nine consecutive years and beating Air Force seven times in that span. Since breaking the forty-three-game losing streak to Notre Dame in 2007, Navy had three wins in the last four games against the Fighting Irish, too.

But all the success—seventy wins and eight straight bowl games since 2003—was making things harder for Navy. When the Mids were a pushover, scheduling games was easy. When Navy couldn't beat the I-AA schools, schools lined up to schedule the Mids for Homecoming, Parents' Weekend or Military Appreciation Day.

But in the Bowl Championship Series (BCS) era, a loss was fatal. So, like a child staring at sweets outside an ice cream shop window, Navy was on the outside looking in on both the big money and small. And scheduling games with a legacy, brand-name school was getting tougher. Getting a home-and-home was next to impossible.

From the 1970s through most of the 2000s, Navy booked home-and-home games with programs like Michigan, Boston College, Syracuse, Virginia or Georgia Tech. The Big East, ACC and even an occasional SEC school on Navy's schedule wasn't uncommon.

But as Johnson's six years ebbed into Niumatalolo's first three seasons, the schedule's punch lessened considerably. A loss was a real possibility when you stepped on the field with the Midshipmen, and fewer schools with national title aspirations were willing to bite.

In Johnson's first year—the "Expect Two Wins" year—Navy played Duke, North Carolina State and Wake Forest (ACC); Northwestern (Big Ten); and Boston College (Big East), plus Army, Air Force and Notre Dame. Now, the schedule was littered by the likes of Northern Illinois, North Texas, Temple, Delaware and Ball State. Games with Rutgers, Pittsburgh and Wake Forest joined Air Force, Notre Dame and Army. But schedules built to entice ticket sales, help recruiting and give Navy a chance to achieve some real splash were no longer easy to produce. Moreover, a marquee name on the schedule was often a byproduct of a one-off quirk in scheduling.

Meanwhile, the money to be made was going to schools in conferences. While the big six conferences (Big Ten, Pac-10, Big 12, Big East, ACC and SEC) hogged 82.3 percent of the $155.2 million paid out by BCS games (in 2009), the Mountain West, Western Athletic Conference, Mid-American Conference, Conference USA and Sun Belt scraped along with the leftovers.[39]

The BCS matched two teams for a national title game, and in 2009, five schools went undefeated, meaning three schools went undefeated and held no hope of playing for the biggest prize. As an independent not named Notre Dame, Navy was staring into an even more uncertain future.

At risk was Navy's continued ability to recruit and play games in the hotbeds it has mined so successfully over the past decade: Florida, Georgia, Tennessee and Texas. When it came to bowl games, geography was important, too. With the exception of the handful of major games that everyone knows—the Rose, Orange and Cotton come to mind quickly— bowls are often a losing proposition when it comes to money.

Detailed at length in *Death to the BCS*, schools big and small lose huge sums of money annually when they accept a post-season bowl invitation. The media report the large payouts bowl games advertise but rarely reveal the overwhelming expenses participating schools agree to take on for the privilege to play the game:

> *To paraphrase Mark Twain, there are three kinds of lies; lies, damned lies and bowl payouts. Bowl games advertise big, flashy payouts, which leaves fans with the impression they're profitable and beneficial for every participating team and part of a positive system that must, at all costs, be preserved.*
>
> *Sorry, but it's all a shell game, a sweetheart deal between the bowls' fat cats and the Cartel that ties all universities to a backward system affecting the Granddaddy of Them All to the Lowliest of Them All. When athletic departments compare actual payouts with expenses, the collective profits are dramatically slimmer than advertised, and the bowl system is more boondoggle than moneymaker. The majority of bowl games leave schools in the red, requiring conferences to pool bowl payouts and take revenue generated by BCS games to cover the losses from lower-tier ones, such as the Motor City Bowl* [now the Little Caesar's Bowl].[40]

All these factors concerned Niumatalolo and Gladchuk greatly. Already working mightily to fill their schedule, Navy was isolated as one of a handful of independents on an island, therefore unable to enjoy two primary advantages a conference membership helps generate: a tie-in system to help place them into a bowl and some protection—strength in numbers, so to speak—to prevent getting soaked by a lower-tier bowl.

*Death to the BCS* detailed the way almost every bowl game milks cash from participating schools by requiring schools to sell a minimum number of game tickets at full price. In 2008, the PapaJohns.com Bowl required Rutgers and North Carolina State to sell 10,000 tickets each. Rutgers moved just 4,650 tickets and absorbed an immediate $214,000 loss from its take. The 2009 Outback Bowl required Iowa and South Carolina to sell 11,000 tickets. Western Michigan ate $450,000 for 11,000 tickets for the 2008 Texas Bowl. Maryland lost $135,000 on tickets for the 2009 Humanitarian Bowl; Ohio State lost $1 million when it sold just 9,983 of a required 17,500 tickets to the 2009 Fiesta Bowl. A year later, the Buckeyes couldn't sell out the Rose Bowl and lost $144,710. Virginia Tech paid full price for 14,158 of a required 17,500 tickets for the 2009 Orange Bowl, resulting in a loss of $1.77 million. The ACC offered an allowance of $1.6 million, but "Va-Tech" spent $3.8 million on the game. The list of schools taking a bath on bowl games is endless, and it wasn't a risk Navy wanted to be exposed to annually.

Because they are the "fleet's team," Navy plays bowl games in or as close to one of its port cities as much as possible. The question to formally pursue a conference affiliation had the potential to fundamentally alter every aspect of the football program, as well as every other team the athletic department oversees.

"Six years ago, you saw a divide happening—you can see it now with the Power 5 and everybody else—[and] we were having a meeting about going into the Big East [because we] had to decide what side we wanted to be on," Niumatalolo said. "It was us going to Chet and the superintendent [Mike Miller] and saying, 'Hey, we've got to get on board or we're going to get left out. And if we get left out, I'm fine with that if you guys are fine with that. If you guys want to go back to I-AA football, I'm cool, but just know things are going to change, so where do you want to be and what side do you want to be on? If you're cool with being over here, I'm cool, but if not, we better try to join one of these leagues.'"

Gladchuk and Miller went to work. On September 22, 2011, the *Baltimore Sun* reported Gladchuk to be in serious discussions with the Big East regarding a potential football-only membership. The same article reported Navy and Air Force were top choices to join the league, citing the Associated Press.

On the field, Navy struggled to the only losing record in the last fourteen years. The Mids opened 2-0 but lost a squeaker at No. 12 South Carolina, 24–21, before the heartbreaking 35–34 loss to Air Force in Annapolis. The hangover from that game snowballed into a six-game losing streak, and the Mids finished 5-7. But the losing record was a one-off; what was happening off the field had the potential to alter Navy football forever.

On January 24, 2012, after almost a year of negotiations, Navy announced that it would join the Big East in football only. After losing Pittsburgh and Syracuse to the ACC and TCU and West Virginia to the Big 12, the Big East was adding Navy, Boise State and San Diego State in football, while SMU, Houston and Central Florida would come aboard in all sports.

Immediately, media, coaches and fans worried if Navy had bitten off more than it could chew. "They signed up to play in the Big East, and all of a sudden Louisville is gone, Pittsburgh is gone, Boise State and San

Navy's Gee Gee Greene stiff-arms the Gamecoks' Marty Markett during the first half of Navy's 24–21 loss to South Carolina. *U.S. Navy/Curtis K. Biasi.*

Diego State are gone," Johnson said, "and with all those teams that were in it when they joined, it would have been a far different cry than the conference they're in."

But Navy was off the hook July 1, 2013, when Louisville, Pittsburgh and Syracuse—schools that played Division I football—left the Big East for the ACC. At the same time, DePaul, Georgetown, Marquette, Providence, St.

John's, Seton Hall and Villanova—I-AA football or Division I basketball schools—took possession of the Big East brand name and the conference's Madison Square Garden tournament contract.

The remaining schools—including Navy and Houston, plus Cincinnati, Connecticut, South Florida and Temple—stayed together in a conference renamed the American Athletic Conference.

During the last ten years of the original Big East's existence, the league was a virtual roulette wheel of schools coming and going. Mike Aresco, formerly the executive vice-president of CBS Sports Programming, was named Big East commissioner on August 14, 2012. His appointment transferred to the AAC. The AAC was a much more manageable proposition for Navy, unlike Army's ill-fated tour in Conference USA from 1998 to 2004. Most important, a conference aligned Navy with four key tenets for the service academy to remain successful.

One was scheduling. It was becoming increasingly difficult to book not just quality opponents but also enough games to fill the schedule. In the BCS era, one loss was a death sentence to a school's national championship hopes. The College Football Playoff era mitigated some of this aversion, but in general, the Power 5 have nothing to gain by scheduling Navy when the likelihood of a loss is real.

A byproduct of scheduling Navy is the commitment it requires to prepare for the triple-option. What Niumatalolo's team can do—create a physical grind that mitigates a talent deficiency unlike any other school in Division I football—is a task most coaches would rather pass on. Instead, they can schedule a Mid-American Conference school (as an example) that runs a similar RPO offense and defense and let their athletic superiority win the game for them.

Second is the television contracts. To no one's surprise, schools are always in search of more revenue and exposure on bigger networks and within better time slots. Since joining the Big Ten, Maryland has benefited greatly from playing on ESPN, ABC or the Big Ten Network (BTN) in the more coveted noon, 3:30 p.m. or evening time slots. Previously, they were regulars at 1:00 p.m. or, worse, 1:30 p.m. in the ACC on a network like Raycom or Jefferson-Pilot. Trying to get someone to leave a noon game for a 1:30 p.m. kickoff is asking a lot, especially when the game isn't on one of the legacy channels.

Also, the Big Ten placed Maryland in the East Division alongside powerhouse brands Michigan, Michigan State, Ohio State and Penn State, making television exposure more advantageous. Navy, by virtue of greater television buying power through a conference instead of as an independent, generates more revenue and exposure, plays in better time slots and overnight was recognized as one of the conference's iconic brands, too.

Third is bowl games, which can wreak havoc on a school's athletic budget. But they're part of the major college football landscape and vitally important to every school's recruiting and fundraising campaigns. Today, every bowl game has a tie-in with a conference, so the days of Navy brokering a bowl game from afar, even a handful of years out, was over. Also, having a conference to help defray the cost of a bowl is a safety net unavailable as an independent.

Finally, and perhaps most importantly (even though it never reaches the critical awareness within mainstream media), there is governance. Unless you're Notre Dame, you're an island unto yourself as an independent when it comes to having a voice—a place at the table, so to speak—within NCAA decision-making. Even Notre Dame, fiercely opposed to sharing money it can produce independently, joined the ACC in all sports except football but partnered with the league to fill five football dates annually for the same reasons.

"If you're not affiliated with a conference, you have no say in the workings of Division I athletics," Gladchuk said. "You're a non-entity, and that's not who Navy is. We're a program of national stature, and we want to be a part of the national landscape and a factor in forming the future of Division I football."

Navy put together a respectable 8-5 record in 2012. The Mids opened in Dublin, Ireland, and were overwhelmed, 50–10, by Notre Dame. The next week, they were manhandled at Penn State, 34–7. Three weeks later, with the season teetering on the brink and trailing at Air Force, 21–13, Niumatalolo subbed in a plebe named Keenan Reynolds for quarterback Trey Miller. The gamble worked, as the Mids rallied for a 28–21 win in overtime. The season saved, Navy ended up 9-4 and the legendary career of No. 19 was launched.

Meanwhile, a bigger victory was in the making behind the Academy walls. There was reluctance to joining the AAC. Would academic and admission standards drop to remain competitive on the football field? Niumatalolo wasn't buying. Navy enjoys one of the highest graduation rates within the NCAA: "The real way that you count it because the NCAA kind of does this bizarre [formula]," Niumatalolo said.

"There's plenty of kids who have great grades and want to play big-time football," Niumatalolo told me. "In recruiting before, we weren't getting

Notre Dame and Navy line up on scrimmage during the Emerald Isle Classic, the season-opening game played in Dublin, Ireland, on September 1, 2012. The Irish pounded Navy, 50–10. *U.S. Navy/Peter D. Lawlor.*

some of those guys, [and] sometimes it's exposure. [But] I wonder if we had set our mark high enough. Duke, Northwestern, Notre Dame, Stanford, Vanderbilt. They sign smart kids, but they can't sign all those players. We don't need to lower our standards."

The Midshipmen kept the CIC in 2013, going 9-4, highlighted by the two service academy games. Despite being thoroughly outplayed in the first half and trailing 10–7, Navy rolled Air Force. Three touchdowns and two interceptions by linebacker Chris Johnson sealed a 28–10 win.

In Philadelphia, Navy whitewashed Army, 34–7. Reynolds dominated in a nasty mix of sleet and snow, and Niumatalolo used the stage to promote his quarterback's Heisman Trophy candidacy for the next season. "I think he deserves to be there.…He's as good a quarterback [as] I've been around," Niumatalolo said to *USA Today*. "Not to take anything away from the guys that are there because of all those guys that are there are very deserving. But I think Keenan had a heck of a year, too."

The 2014 season opened with the Midshipmen hosting No. 8 Ohio State in Baltimore, and turnovers—mostly unforced mistakes—cost Navy any chance at a possible upset.

For the second straight year, Keenan Reynolds was Most Valuable Player of the Army-Navy game, here scoring Navy's second touchdown in a 34–7 win, the Mids' twelfth in a row in the series. *U.S. Navy/Marvin Lynchard.*

Ohio State hemmed in Navy's best efforts during a 34–17 win in Baltimore in 2014. A handful of unforced Navy mistakes in the middle stages of the game made a Navy comeback impossible. *U.S. Navy/Nathan A. Wilkes.*

The Midshipmen celebrate the 44–28 victory over Pittsburgh in the 2015 Military Bowl at Navy–Marine Corps Memorial Stadium, giving Navy a school-record eleven wins for the season. *U.S. Navy/ EJ Hersom.*

The next week, the Buckeyes were stunned by Virginia Tech in Columbus, 35–21, but instead of focusing on what Ohio State did wrong against the Hokies, Cleveland.com's Doug Lesmerises focused on how playing Navy the previous week contributed to the Virginia Tech loss: "Since 2009, when Ohio State played the first game of this two-game Navy series, 18 power conference opponents have played Navy one week and come back against a major college opponent the next week….Those 17 teams are 8-10 in the week after the Midshipmen."[41]

No longer a feel-good story, the commentary demonstrated the change in how national media viewed Niumatalolo and his Midshipmen. By 2015, Reynolds's final season, almost every Navy record within his reach fell to his name. Navy's 11-2 record was the first eleven-win season in program history. The Mids swamped Air Force, 33–11, and No. 15 and undefeated Memphis, 45–20, in the Liberty Bowl. The win over the Tigers was notable because it was the first win over a ranked team in eighteen years, and it happened on national television. When the team arrived back at the yard at 4:00 a.m., the majority of the Brigade was up to greet them, with lights flashing and music playing. After taking down Army, 17–13, the Mids overwhelmed Pittsburgh in the Military Bowl, 44–28.

# THE HEISMAN SNUB

As a senior, Reynolds had marched Navy to a 9-2 record entering the Army game in Philadelphia and had a Heisman Trophy–quality season himself. Inexplicably, he was excluded as a finalist for the award, and the lead-up to his omission triggered a national debate. On December 10, Tom Pedulla of the *New York Times* wrote a feature detailing the lengths a primary stakeholder and the award's broadcasting partner, ESPN, went to exclude the best player Navy had produced in well over a generation.

Within that article, Pedulla wrote of how, after Navy's 51–31 loss at Houston eliminated the Mids from playing in the inaugural AAC title game, Reynolds was dropped by ESPN as one of the five listed candidates in online voting at the award's promotional website, titled the Nissan Heisman House. What made that decision dubious was the fact that Reynolds was leading the fan voting by a substantial margin. With Reynolds dropped, Alabama tailback Derrick Henry quickly made up a twelve-point deficit to draw even.

Reynolds was later restored after Navy's Sports Information Department and U.S. Senator John McCain (R-Arizona), a 1958 Navy grad, took to Twitter to lead a nation's collective displeasure. ESPN responded to the significant criticism from many media outlets and restored Reynolds's name after enough fans continued with an arduous write-in campaign. Ultimately, Reynolds won the fan vote, overcoming his twelve-point lead being taken from him to claim 38 percent of the vote to Henry's 34 percent. That forced Nissan, the award's title sponsor, to cast its lone vote for Reynolds.

But by the time the finalists were announced on December 6, the damage had been done: Henry, Stanford tailback Christian McCaffrey and Clemson quarterback Deshaun Watson were the only players invited. The Navy team, which had hustled into a meeting room following practice to watch the finalist announcement, sat in stunned silence at the snub.

"If Keenan Reynolds is not a Heisman finalist they need to change the Heisman mission statement to the most outstanding college football player in a single season that plays in a [Power 5] conference," Navy Sports Information Director Scott Strasemeier snarked to the *Capital-Gazette* moments after the announcement. "It's a shame Keenan didn't get invited, because he deserved it. Not because he played at Navy, but because over the last four years he's been the best player in college football."

Strasemeier's commentary was correct but also pointed to a possible reason why Reynolds was omitted. With 1,093 yards and nineteen touchdowns rushing, plus another 964 yards and six touchdowns passing entering the Army game, his 2015 stats didn't leap off the page like Henry's 2,219 rushing yards and twenty-eight touchdowns.

For a player looking to crash the annual New York City party, this requirement was a hurdle Reynolds couldn't overcome, but still, his overt exclusion was odd considering the Heisman Trophy's own description celebrates a player "whose performance best exhibits the pursuit of excellence with integrity." On the day of the Heisman presentation, Reynolds became the first Navy quarterback to beat Army four times, and during the 2015 season, Reynolds became the NCAA's career leader in rushing yards by a quarterback (4,559) and rushing touchdowns (eighty-eight). If that's not pursuing excellence, what is?

The snub also scuttled the need to scramble two helicopters to take a nine-person contingent from the field in Philadelphia to New York City, eliminating what would have been the most dramatic Heisman Trophy presentation entrance ever. Henry won the award, taking 1,832 points of the vote. With 180 points, Reynolds finished fifth, but he outpaced LSU's Leonard Fournette, Ohio State's Ezekiel Elliott and Michigan State's Connor Cook, who was MSU's winningest quarterback in school history and the winner of the Johnny Unitas Award.

Losing a player like Reynolds would cripple most programs, evidenced by Michigan State's 3-9 record in 2016 after losing Cook following three years with a combined record of 36-5, but in 2016, Navy enjoyed a season that can only be described as enchanting. Having qualified to host the AAC title game, with the Army game to follow, they found themselves on the cusp of the Cotton Bowl, until the Mids finally faltered after overcoming remarkable obstacles that challenged the team all season long.

No 9-5 team in college football history ever stood to earn a spot in the Cotton Bowl, but the New Year's Day game's matchup was being held up on December 3, when the Mids hosted Temple in the AAC title game. Western Michigan, already 13-0, had to wait to see if Navy could snatch the lone New Year's Day appointment afforded the Group of 5 from the Broncos.

Tasked with replacing thirty-six seniors, including Reynolds and nine other offensive starters, Navy rattled off eight straight wins to enter the Top 25 for the second time in 2016, at No. 18. Against FCS Fordham in the opener, starting quarterback Tago Smith went down with an ACL injury. Worth came in, and with third-string quarterback Zach Abey unavailable due to an honor code violation, the coaches had to run into the stands and find freshman Malcolm Perry, who would change out of his dress whites and into his football uniform. He played, rushing seven times for thirty yards in

Navy's 52–16 win. "I'm not sure if a guy's ever come out of the Brigade in the middle of a game and gone in to play…ever," Pete Medhurst, Navy's play-by-play radio voice, told his audience of the unique move. Navy's Sports Information Department took a lighthearted jab at the moment, too, tweeting: "More national media tweeting about our fourth string [*sic*] QB than they did about 11 win Navy team last year."

It would be a common refrain; the Midshipmen suffered more injuries than any FBS school. However, Smith's injury would open a door for Worth, and he quickly became a local legend and household name nationally.

Over the next ten weeks, the former third-string quarterback and placeholder became the nation's leader in rushing touchdowns (twenty-five) and thirty-three overall. North set the Navy single-season record for total yards with 2,595.

Inside the locker room, Worth was as respected and accomplished off the field as any Midshipman. That he had plied his trade, waited his turn and then exploded when given his chance made him a rock star among his teammates. "He's such a good guy, and such a great Midshipman, he's the only person at the Academy I'd let sleep with my sister," one teammate said, requesting anonymity for obvious reasons. Said Alohi Gilman, "We called Will our next President, or we'd tell him he's the future Supe of the Academy, but he really is a great guy, and he was a great leader for the team."

Worth's success was all part of the larger, dramatic and unexplainable dynamic that trademarked Navy's season. In a 28–24 win over Connecticut, the Mids ran out to a 21–0 lead, fell behind 24–21 and then reclaimed the lead on Worth's touchdown with 3:08 left. The final two plays were breathtaking. First, a back shoulder pass from Bryce Shiffeffs had Hergy Mayala on the doorstep of a touchdown, but Gilman forced Mayala out at the one-yard line. It turned out to be a huge play, because on the snap, the Huskies had no timeouts but inexplicably called for a run play. Navy stuffed Ron Johnson short of the goal line, and the clock ran out. "They pulled their left guard and tried to run the ball over the right C gap, and we just got enough hats on the ball to stop it," Gilman said. "I remember the coaches telling us to take our time getting off the pile, and if you look at the replay, one of our linebackers literally shoves our D-lineman to keep him down until the clock ran out."

When the Mids pulled the season's biggest upset, a 46–40 win over No. 6 Houston in rain-soaked Annapolis, video of Houston's final lateral pass skidding out of bounds followed by the Midshipmen storming the field had Navy football trending in the top spot on Twitter. An improbable goal line stand and a late fumble recovery punctuated a 42–28 win over Memphis on homecoming.

During the second half of the Mids' 28–27 win over Notre Dame in Jacksonville, Navy held the ball for almost twenty-one minutes but still needed two fourth-down conversions in the final four minutes to secure the win. This game, like so many others, showcased Navy's discipline. In 2016, the Mids averaged just 2.8 penalties per game—incurring just thirty-nine fouls and 341 yards in fourteen games.

Navy's rise was so notable that it kick-started a discussion within national media and even a few coaches and athletic directors, mostly from the schools lumped in the so-called Group of 5—a playoff and/or championship separate of the Power 5 conferences.

With wins over two Big Ten schools, Illinois and Northwestern, Western Michigan's 13-0 record was impressive. Their problem was that the Broncos' only other signature win was a 45–31 win over 7-6 Eastern Michigan, which hadn't recorded a winning record since 1995 and played in a bowl game for the first time since 1987.

Meanwhile, Navy's 9-2 record included wins over No. 6 Houston, Notre Dame and eight straight victories to reach the AAC title game. The rankings came out on the Tuesday before Navy's game with Temple, and besides the playoff slots, all the bowl pairings had been announced… except the Cotton Bowl.

It was obvious that the playoff committee was holding the trip to Dallas from WMU to see if Navy could run the table and end the season 11-2. Navy's two-loss season in the AAC could trump WMU's undefeated season in the MAC. But the season ended with three crushing defeats. A 34–10 loss to Temple in the second AAC title game preceded Army's first win in fifteen seasons, 21–17 in Baltimore. The Mids accepted an invitation to the Armed Forces Bowl, to which they had previously committed, sans an invite to a New Year's Day bowl. Western Michigan ended up in the Cotton Bowl, where it deserved to go after an undefeated season.

The Mids lost the Armed Forces Bowl to Louisiana Tech, 52–45, but the ending aside, 2016 was perhaps one of the most captivating seasons in Naval Academy history.


Later in December, Northern Illinois Athletic Director Sean Frazier declared that "the time to have a realistic conversation" about a non–Power 5 playoff was at hand, saying discussions about how to put such a playoff in place had already happened. It grabbed the attention of media and coaches immediately. Was this real? It had to be if a Mid-American Conference athletic director—with one of his conference's schools about to play the Cotton Bowl—was willing to make such comments.

The College Football Playoff, just three years old, hadn't seen a Group of 5 school qualify for the football version of the "Final Four," and of the twelve spots for the six New Year's Day games, just one slot is afforded to the schools from the Group of 5.

After the season, with Tom Herman leaving Houston for the job at Texas, Yahoo! Sports called Niumatalolo the most recognizable coach among the Group of 5 schools. Navy had been standing on the same doorstep with Western Michigan, poised to snatch the diamond from the Broncos despite their perfect record. Niumatalolo bluntly shot down the idea of a separate playoff when asked by the *Capital-Gazette* newspaper on March 21, 2017: "I'm not into that."

Niumatalolo addressed the AAC's push to be considered more with the Power 5 conferences of the ACC, Big Ten, Big 12, Pac-12 and SEC than with the likes of Conference USA and the Sun Belt. AAC Commissioner Mike Aresco tried to coin the term "Power 6" and said in October that the league would "ramp up" its efforts on the labeling front if the Big 12 didn't take any AAC schools in expansion.

Wins over teams like Oklahoma and other Power 5 conferences will do more than a marketing push. "We have this discussion. We'll have it in May [at conference meetings] with all the AAC coaches and we'll have the marketing people come in and try to show us the new logo for the AAC and the TV people come in and do all that," Niumatalolo said. "We've got to win. Bottom line for our conference, we've got to beat people out of conference. We've got to beat Power 5 schools. And I think what's happened is our conference is doing that and I think the more and more we can do that, hopefully it can get us in that discussion."

To no one's surprise, MAC Commissioner John Steinbrecher rebuked the comments of Frazier, who had broken ranks, by mirroring Niumatalolo's comments. "The logistical ability of doing a [separate playoff] is, from where I'm sitting, almost impossible," Steinbrecher said.

"Now the dean of the Group of 5 coaches, Niumatalolo was reported by USA Today to be making $2 million in 2016, double of Monken ($932,521) and Calhoun ($885,000) and still $182,000 more than what his service rivals made combined. This was the culmination of Gladchuk's goal when he took the job in 2001—to ensure Navy's coaches earned compensation in the top half of the college football industry. Niumatalolo's salary was 57th of 128 coaches.

These numbers pale in comparison to Michigan's Jim Harbaugh, reportedly the nation's highest-salaried coach at $9,004,000, according to *USA Today*.

Niumatalolo's pay reveals a healthy reward for the success he's steered. In 2008, NAAA's 990 form showed Niumatalolo making $896,352 in reportable income; in 2010, that number jumped to $1,577,399—a base of $1,238,371 and a bonus of up to $265,000, payable at Gladchuk's discretion."

Niumatalolo was courted heavily in 2015 and listened long enough to have BYU offer him the job, but he decided to stay at Navy. In 2016, Niumatalolo hired a new agent, leaving Beard for agent Lee Kaplan at the Legacy Agency, after being courted by Thayer Evans, a former investigative reporter for *Sports Illustrated*. None of the buzz amounted to much worry in Annapolis that Niumatalolo would leave.

## ALOHA, ALOHI

A different departure stung Navy in the spring of 2017. Quietly, Navy has enjoyed immense success recruiting top-shelf, under-the-radar talent during the Johnson-Niumatalolo era. It was exposed when the Department of Defense changed course, and it might have cost the Midshipmen a sophomore with outstanding potential.

On April 26, 2017, one day before the NFL Draft, Air Force's Jalen Robinette learned that the Air Force would not honor requests from Cadets to join the Ready Reserve if they signed a professional sports contract. Robinette expected to be selected and have an opportunity like the one Reynolds took on with the Baltimore Ravens following the 2016 Commissioning Ceremony in Annapolis.

Skittish to waste a pick on a player who could not perform due to military commitment, all thirty NFL teams passed on Robinette, who tweeted defiantly against the decision on April 29: "You're out of your mind if you think I'm gonna let someone else hang up my cleats. Momma raised me better than that."

Curiously, Gilman retweeted Robinette's post. After spending the 2015 season at the Naval Academy Preparatory School (NAPS) in Rhode Island, Gilman had an outstanding season as a freshman. He played in all fourteen games, starting twelve at three different positions: outside linebacker, corner and strong safety. He finished second on the team with seventy-six tackles, five passes defended and a fumble recovery for a touchdown in the UConn game. Gilman was named the Eastern Collegiate Athletic Conference Rookie of the Year and an Honorable Mention All-AAC selection.

On April 29, the Department of Defense formally ended its deferred duty policy for professional athletes in a memo, canceling an edict dating back to May 5, 2016. Less than a year old, the deferred duty policy had been hailed positively in an expansive, eight-page feature titled "Patriot Games" by Andrew Lawrence in the January 23, 2017 edition of *Sports Illustrated*.

Evidenced by a handful of subsequent tweets, Gilman's tenor and tone on Twitter had changed. On May 10, Gilman tweeted, "I wouldn't have changed a thing if I had a chance." Why was Gilman, a sophomore who was expected to be one of Navy's top defenders in 2017, talking about changing anything? On May 31, the other shoe dropped when he announced on Twitter that he was transferring from the Naval Academy, writing in an attached note that "my goals and passions are not the best fit with the Naval Academy." On June 1, Gilman told the *Capital-Gazette*, "I definitely have some options. I consider myself a Division I scholarship player."

He did, although he didn't confirm it until June 9. Notre Dame had offered Gilman a full scholarship the day he was released from the Academy, and he had accepted. Irish coach Brian Kelly, likely impressed by Gilman's twelve tackles in Navy's win over Notre Dame, outmaneuvered Southern Cal for Gilman's services. While it left a hole in Navy's defense, it also showed how much Navy had closed the talent deficit it was facing under Weatherbie in the late 1990s. Gilman is believed to be the first player to ever transfer from Navy to Notre Dame, begging the question: how many other "under the radar" guys are there at Navy?

"There's a lot," Gilman said. "They don't get the highest-ranked recruits, but they get a lot of under-the-radar guys like me, Will Worth…guys that can contribute on a high-level team."

And what about playing Navy in the future—how awkward might that be? "I told some of my teammates about the Notre Dame offer, and they were very supportive of me and my decision, so it'll be interesting to line up against Navy," Gilman said. "I absolutely loved my experience playing for Navy. The brotherhood there is easily the greatest thing I've ever been a part of…my main priority was to make sure that I left on good terms with the boys I grinded with at Navy."

Obviously, his transfer stung. The Naval Academy had seen promise in him and committed two years to his improvement, the first at NAPS, where he met Myles Benning, a fullback from Carrollton, Texas. Benning knew immediately how big the loss was. "I knew he was transferring before anyone, two days before he announced, and I knew he was offered a full scholarship by Notre Dame as soon as he was released from the academy," Benning said. "Besides being one of my best friends on the team, the bond you form being on the team together at Navy is something you hear a lot about when you're recruited, but it becomes so much more real when things like this happen. We're going to miss him as a team, but I wish him the best."

While admitting that the Department of Defense decision "definitely took away an opportunity for me to pursue a passion of mine," Gilman said he had been considering a transfer as far back as January. Niumatalolo's comments about Gilman's transfer to the *Capital-Gazette*, however, lent more credibility to the idea that that DoD decision had helped snatch him from the Mids, as he wished Gilman luck in "pursuing his NFL dreams."

His decision begged the question: would Gilman's outstanding numbers as a freshman at Navy, such as his fifty solo tackles, five tackles for loss and two fumble recoveries, translate to Notre Dame? There's a huge difference between playing schools like South Florida, Connecticut and Memphis at Navy as opposed to Georgia, Southern Cal and Stanford at Notre Dame.

It further illustrated that Navy isn't a meathead warehouse and that football is always secondary to the mission of the Academy, no matter how much more competitive the Blue and Gold become. Reynolds's Heisman snub and Gilman's transfer are primary examples of that differential.

While Gilman's Navy door closed, Tom O'Brien's reopened. The former Midshipman, who sought the head coach's job at Navy before both the 1990 and 1995 seasons—and ran afoul of the Academy as the coach at Boston College—came back home to join Pete Medhurst on the football broadcasts as a color analyst. Life is full of second chances, and his hiring represented a favorite son coming home.

Entering the fall of 2017, Navy is a well-oiled machine. No one runs around the offices of Ricketts Hall like a chicken with its head cut off. There's no need for wasted motion. After fifteen years of winning consistently, the coaches and administrators anticipate situations and responses when it comes to the schedule, opponents, the offensive and defensive systems and, most importantly, recruiting.

That's why a player like Worth, a third-string backup and placekicking holder you likely never heard of before September 3, 2016, comes off the bench in the season opener, plays ten games and rewrites a healthy portion of Navy's single-season record book.

"There is no end chapter to our book," Gladchuk said. "As long as I'm here, we're going to keep winning. When Paul Johnson inherited a team that won just two games, we expected to win. When he left for Georgia Tech and Kenny Niumatalolo took over, we expected to win. Nothing has changed....We're going to continue to win."

# UNFORGETTABLE GAMES

## OCTOBER 8, 2016: NAVY 46, NO. 6 HOUSTON 40

A multimillion-dollar loss. That's what Navy handed No. 6 Houston in major college football's biggest upset of the season.

The Cougars opened 2016 by thrashing No. 3 Oklahoma on national television, 33–23, putting them in position to go undefeated and win their league title, crash the College Football Playoff as a playoff qualifier and leave the American Athletic Conference for the Big 12 Conference, where licensing, media rights, television contracts and other revenue would expand exponentially.

With Houston coach Tom Herman already a hot commodity by being linked to a handful of potential openings, the specter of the Cougars joining the Big 12 was palpable. The Midshipmen, meanwhile, were seventeen-point underdogs after a 28–14 loss to Air Force the week before and were starting last year's third-string quarterback, Will Worth.

But during the pregame warm-up, Houston players mocked Navy's two captains, Tago Smith and Daniel Gonzalez, for limping on immobilizing carts. "Our guys came in the locker room [before the run-out] seeing red," Niumatalolo said. "Usually, you don't want guys getting caught up in that kind of stuff, but our guys were fired up."

Navy racked up 306 yards rushing against a defense that surrendered an average of just 42 per game. Worth ran for 115 yards and passed for 76 yards and two touchdowns, both in the second half. The first was a 17-yard strike to Darryl Bonner out of the backfield, putting Navy up, 27–20. On the next possession, Josiah Powell picked off Houston quarterback Greg Ward Jr. and raced 34 yards for the game-changing score.

Worth's second touchdown pass, a thirty-four-yard strike to Brandon Colon, put Navy up, 41–27. A field goal and safety clinched the Mids' first win over a Top 10 team since 1984.

Houston had won eighteen straight games that Ward started, the longest such streak in FBS, but his Heisman Trophy candidacy was ruined by two interceptions and a fumble, leading to seventeen points for Navy, which didn't commit a turnover.

The game ended with a series of laterals—the Cougars' final pitch missed badly and skidded into the Navy sideline—and the Brigade stormed off the risers and onto the field. Every national highlight package led with the game's result, and the @NavyFB handle dominated social media feeds, trending in the No. 1 position nationally for hours after the upset.

# OCTOBER 6, 2012: NAVY 28, AIR FORCE 21 (OT)

Daring and desperate. That best describes Ken Niumatalolo's decision to sit junior quarterback Trey Miller for an unknown plebe while staring at an eight-point deficit in the fourth quarter of the 2012 Air Force game. In a matter of minutes, the career of Keenan Reynolds, a freshman from Antioch, Tennessee, who had been heavily recruited by Air Force, was afoot. Navy football would never be the same.

Coming off a 5-7 season in 2011, the Midshipmen limped into Colorado Springs, Colorado, with a 1-3 record as nine-point underdogs. An unusual 9:40 a.m. kickoff left ice falling from television camera zip lines. Ground fog rose from the turf at kickoff.

The fifteen previous Air Force–Navy games had decided the winner of the Commander-in-Chief Trophy. The Falcons scored first and were on the move again when the Mids' Tra'ves Bush scooped an Air Force fumble at the Mids' twenty-seven, setting up a five-yard touchdown by fullback Noah Copeland to make it 10–7, Navy.

But Navy's momentum evaporated, and Air Force surged ahead, 14–10, with thirty-seven seconds left in the third quarter. Miller was leading the charge back until he tweaked his left ankle while scrambling unsuccessfully to convert a third-and-9. He rushed for 110 yards to that point but had to be helped to the sideline.

Nick Sloan booted a forty-one-yard field goal to make it 14–13 with about ten minutes to play as Niumatalolo wondered what to do. "Miller said he was good to go, but I guess it wasn't the emphatic answer I was looking for," Niumatalolo said. "So I told Ivin [Jasper], 'Let's go with Reynolds and see if he sparks us.'"

Two plays later, Dontae Strickland's fifty-four-yard option pass found Drew Coleman's arms to put Air Force up, 21–13, with 9:13 left. "I was numb," Reynolds said. "It's a huge game, we're on the road, we're down, and they're asking me—a lowly freshman—to go in and make a play."

Reynolds marched Navy seventy-five yards, scoring from fifteen out to bring the Mids within 21–19 before making a critical mistake. "On that two-point try, I made the wrong read by pitching Noah the ball," Reynolds said. "He should have been tackled in the backfield. Instead, he made a spectacular play and got in the end zone."

Parker Herrington's second missed field goal sailed left on the final play of regulation to give Navy new life, but during the first possession, Reynolds fumbled a snap into the end zone. Guard Jake Zuzek recovered to put Navy up, 27–21. "Noah should have been tackled, but he wasn't," Reynolds said. "I fumbled the snap, but Jake recovers the ball. There was a feeling of divine intervention because things just fell into place."

When defensive end Wes Henderson batted down Connor Dietz's fourth-down pass, Navy's most improbable win in the contentious rivalry kicked off a wild celebration. Later that season, Reynolds led Navy past Army when the Cadets' Trent Steelman infamously fumbled at Navy's fourteen-yard line. The Mids recovered with just over a minute left.

Four years and thirty-five wins later, including a 7-1 record versus Army and Air Force, the greatest quarterback in Navy's modern-day history had his number, 19, retired—the first active Midshipman so honored since Napoleon McCallum. "Ironic, huh? My first bit of real playing time happens at Air Force?" Reynolds said. "We were 1-3, coming off a 5-7 season.... Those were some very gloomy days. We went on to win six of the next seven games. Our season and our program changed forever."

# OCTOBER 23, 2010: NAVY 35, NOTRE DAME 17

Because the series means much more to the Midshipmen, any Navy victory over Notre Dame earns consideration on a list of greatest Navy wins.

But unlike any other win—there's only been thirteen in ninety games—2010 was a coronation, cementing Navy's return to major college football. The Mids devastated Notre Dame like few Navy teams ever have. Free safety Wyatt Middleton, one of Navy's captains, exuded confidence in the locker room minutes before kickoff. "As individuals, we might be nervous, but as a team? We solid, baby!" Middleton barked with immense bravado before leaving with Ricky Dobbs for the coin toss. "I'll see you boys out there!"

That it came on the heels of a pair of two-point victories over the Irish in the previous three years made it even more improbable. There was no way Notre Dame could've overlooked or underestimated their Annapolis rivals.

But if there was any doubt, standing in the locker room of the Meadowlands, a billion-dollar edifice to modern stadia, Niumatalolo knew exactly what to say to take the pressure of playing the bigger, faster and more highly recruited Irish away from his team. "Nine years ago, not very far from here, the face of our country and the face of our world changed, and you guys answered the call!" Niumatalolo intoned. "I couldn't be more proud or more blessed to be with a bunch of brothers like you. Regardless of the course of this game, I love you guys. Let's go have some fun!"

And they did. The Midshipmen snuffed out Notre Dame's first possession at the goal line on fourth down and a foot to go, and the momentum of the play kick-started the rout. "We outman them by 70 pounds on average up front," Kelly told the Associated Press. "If you can't get a foot on the one-half yard line, you get what you deserve."

Alexander Teich ran for an astounding 210 yards, becoming the first Navy fullback to reach the 200-yard mark in a game. Quarterback Ricky Dobbs scored three times and threw a touchdown (to, who else, Teich), as Navy rolled up 367 rushing, the most ever laid down by the Mids on Notre Dame.

With Navy holding a 35–10 lead with 4:38 left in the third quarter, the Associated Press described the surreal scene best: "It was a Navy home game at the NFL stadium, but there were plenty of Notre Dame fans in the crowd of 75,614—and plenty heading for the exits when the third quarter ended."

The *Chicago Tribune* called Navy's win "overpowering," while Notre Dame coach Brian Kelly admitted to the paper, "Navy was the better football team." That's generous. It wasn't even that close.

The eighteen-point difference was the largest win margin since the 35–14 victory in 1963. Speaking of the Joe Bellino–Roger Staubach era, it was Navy's third victory over Notre Dame in four years, something that hadn't happened since 1960–63.

The 1937, 1964 and 2011 classes are the only ones in Navy history to own three wins over Notre Dame. Niumatalolo might have enjoyed the noisy crescendo of stomping the Irish in a game that wasn't as close as the score indicated, but gloating was never his style. "The Notre Dame wins are always huge, because we haven't beat them very often," Niumatalolo admitted, "but out of all the Notre Dame wins, the one for me is the Meadowlands, because it wasn't a fluke. It wasn't, 'We barely won…' We got after them pretty good."

## NOVEMBER 1, 2008: NAVY 33, TEMPLE 27

Russ Pospisil couldn't believe that Temple tried to run the football. Clint Sovie didn't think—he just grabbed the ball and ran as fast as he could. The greatest fourth-quarter comeback in Navy history should never have happened. The Midshipmen were down 27–7 with about nine minutes to play. They'd scraped to within a touchdown, but Temple had the ball and Navy couldn't stop the clock with a minute left.

Inexplicably, Temple ran the ball. Kee-ayre Griffin coughed it up an instant before he went down. Pospisil, the linebacker who jarred the ball free from Griffin's grip, watched as Sovie, also a linebacker, did the rest, scooping the ball and racing forty-two yards for the touchdown. "I was surprised they ran it…thank God they did," Pospisil told the Associated Press, while Sovie said, "I thought he was down. I just saw the ball, picked it up and started running." The improbable score tied the game, and Navy stole the victory in overtime, 33–27.

The comeback was remarkable for other reasons, too. First, the victory made Navy 6-3, eligible to accept the invitation to a bowl game in Niumatalolo's first season. The game also launched the career of quarterback Ricky Dobbs, then a third-string backup to Kaipo-Noa Kaheaku-Enhada.

The prospects of victory were beyond bleak. Kaheaku-Enhada re-injured a hamstring with three minutes left in the third quarter, but Niumatalolo continued to spur his troops and Dobbs suddenly caught fire. Taking over on his own twenty-two, Dobbs drove the Mids down to

Temple's twenty-two before firing a strike down the seam to wideout T.J. Thiel for a touchdown. On Navy's next possession, Dobbs drove Navy sixty-four yards to Temple's one. He called his own number but was stuffed at the line. Improvising before he was tackled, he pitched to Eric Kettani, who bulldozed in to make it 27–20 with 2:52 left.

In position to run the clock out, the Owls could have kneeled on the clock and punted. When the ball popped out, Sovie was on the football so fast that players and fans alike weren't certain what they were seeing was real. "Honestly, everybody's running down the sideline, and I'm standing there like, 'Did [Sovie] really do that?'" Kettani told the *Washington Post*.

In overtime, Navy staged a goal line stand, stopping Griffin at the one on third down and then watching as Adam DiMichele's pass, potentially his fourth touchdown of the game, was dropped by Steve Maneri. Poised to steal the outcome, Dobbs drove the Mids from the twenty-five- to the one-yard line before breaking the plane of the goal line while running to the left.

The Midshipmen poured off the sideline in jubilation; the Owls walked away in disconsolate silence, unable to muster an explanation for an unthinkable loss. "Certainly, we could have kneeled down....We thought that would have taken the clock down to 18 or 19 seconds, and then you punt it away," Temple coach Al Golden told the *Post*. "I don't question that decision."

## NOVEMBER 3, 2007: NAVY 46, NOTRE DAME 44 (3 OT)

The night "the Streak" died—the longest losing streak in NCAA history—eighty thousand fans at Notre Dame Stadium watched in stunned silence as Navy let go of forty-three years of misery, embarrassment and frustration.

There were tears and hugs, and primal screams seared through the night. If the music died in Chicago, this is how the forty-three-game losing streak died in South Bend, Indiana. It's a moment in the program's history that will never be forgotten by the thousands of Academy graduates and Navy football fans who watched it in person and around the world.

The picture frozen in time—"Navy 46, Notre Dame 44" on the stadium scoreboard, silhouetted against that classic midwestern autumn sunset—is found hanging in countless offices, restaurants, bars and barbershops around Annapolis, as if it happened a week ago. The Streak hung around the neck of the program like an anchor, and it was dispatched in epic, cathartic fashion. Does a losing streak that spans more than four decades die any other way?

With the score tied at 28 and forty-five seconds remaining, Notre Dame coach Charlie Weis inexplicably decided against trying a forty-one-yard field goal, instead opting for a fourth-and-eight from Navy's twenty-four-yard line. But linebacker Ram Vela leapt over his blocker on the end and launched like a missile into quarterback Evan Sharpley, while Chris Kuhar-Pitters—who earlier scooped and scored a fumble from sixteen yards out—thundered past the offensive line and hauled Sharpley down to guarantee overtime.

The game-winning score was Kaipo-Noa Kaheaku-Enhada's twenty-five-yard touchdown pass to Reggie Campbell, tucked inside the right front pylon, on the first play of the third overtime. Campbell caught the two-point conversion, too.

On Notre Dame's final possession, a five-yard touchdown by Travis Thomas, plus a pass-interference call on the two-point try, threatened to send the game into a fourth set of possessions. But Navy's Michael Welsh and Irv Spencer pulled down Thomas short of the goal line on the second try.

Bedlam ensued. The Mids thundered onto the field. Navy play-by-play man Bob Socci described the play on WNAV like this:

> *The Irish with the football at the 1…a 2-point try looming after a questionable pass-interference call. Navy leads by two in triple overtime. In motion, the tight end, right to left…Sharpley pulls away, hands it to Travis Thomas…runs it RIGHT SIDE! HE'LL BE STOPPED! AND SO WILL A 43-GAME LOSING STREAK FOR NAVY AGAINST NOTRE DAME! Four decades-plus of frustration and futility, of lopsided losses and narrow defeats for the Midshipmen…all are forgotten on a 2-point-conversion run by Travis Thomas…stuffed in the backfield by the Midshipmen!*

In Annapolis, bars everywhere swelled in celebration. It was like Mardi Gras, Game 7 of the World Series and the Super Bowl all unexpectedly rolled into one night. Midshipmen took high-fives from complete strangers passing on the sidewalks and red bricks. A full weekend liberty for the entire Brigade was declared, and classes were canceled for the coming Monday.

Back in South Bend, Christian Swezey of the *Washington Post* described the on-field post-game scene like this:

*Flashbulbs popped in the dark night as the jubilant Navy football team congregated in front of its drum-and-bugle corps for the playing of the alma mater.....Nearby, Notre Dame's players and coaches stood quietly and watched. It was a historic moment, and one that belonged solely to the Midshipmen.*

The night the Streak died...

## DECEMBER 25, 1996: NAVY 42, CALIFORNIA 38 (ALOHA BOWL)

To get its first win in a bowl game in nearly twenty years, Navy used two fourth-quarter touchdowns—sandwiching a fumble recovery with less than two minutes to play deep in its territory  to stun Coach Steve Mariucci's Bears.

Memorable for a number of reasons, the Aloha Bowl is remembered for Navy racking up an astounding 646 yards, including 479 through the first three quarters. Obviously, it wasn't enough to stop Coach Charlie Weatherbie from making a change at quarterback. Chris McCoy, whose name remains omnipresent in the Navy record books, led Navy to 479 yards in total offense entering the fourth quarter. But Weatherbie tapped Ben Fay, and he responded by rushing for a pair of touchdowns.

After scoring thirty-five points in the first half, Cal managed just a field goal in the second, allowing Navy to storm back. The game-winning score, a ten-yard scamper by Fay, came with 1:19 to play.

But like most stirring comebacks, there's a pair of significant what-ifs: What if Weatherbie hadn't replaced McCoy with Fay? What if Cal quarterback Pat Barnes hadn't been stripped of the ball by David Viger and recovered at Navy's sixteen-yard line by Jerome Dixon with less than two minutes to play? "If you make that decision and it doesn't work, you become the guy who lost the game," said Niumatalolo, who was a position coach in 1996. "It worked out brilliantly, so everyone felt like a hero."

Ironically, Niumatalolo would make a similar decision as head coach in 2012, replacing junior quarterback Trey Miller for a plebe named Keenan Reynolds in the fourth quarter of a dogfight with Air Force. Navy trailed, 21–13, at the time of the change but went on to defeat the Falcons, 28–21, in overtime.

McCoy and Fay combined to complete fourteen of twenty-one passes for 395 yards—huge numbers for an option first team—while Navy ran fifty times for 251 yards. Two turnovers in the third quarter stymied the Mids' attack, and when McCoy continued to struggle, Fay took center stage with 10:38 to play.

The Aloha Bowl win was the crescendo of a season that included narrow losses to Boston College (43–28) and Army (28–24). But Weatherbie poured water on the idea Navy had missed achieving better overall results. "We were 5-6 [in 1995] and probably should have won three or four more games, and then we were 9-3 (in 1996) and probably should have lost three or four close games," Weatherbie said. "We found a way to win the bowl game because a lot of guys stepped up and made a couple plays. Team always wins first."

## NOVEMBER 17, 1984:
## NAVY 38, NO. 2 SOUTH CAROLINA 21

Navy's most infamous upset is an unexplainable result that thirty years later still evokes anger and frustration in Columbia, South Carolina. It's a wound that has never fully healed. And don't let the final score fool you—it wasn't that close. With ten minutes left in the fourth quarter, Navy was rolling, 38–7.

Holding an unexpected 14–7 halftime lead, the Midshipmen exploded for the next twenty-four points, including a seventeen-point flurry in the third quarter. Brian Clouse and Mike Smith, two running backs Navy coach Gary Tranquill described as "pipsqueaks" to reporters after the game, did the most damage. Smith scored twice and totaled ninety-six yards, while Clouse scored on a fifty-three-yard run in the third and had ninety-seven yards on twelve carries.

Navy was missing Heisman Trophy candidate Napoleon McCallum, who broke his ankle in the second game of the season. Quarterback Bill Byrne broke his leg in an 18–17 loss to Notre Dame. John Berner, the other starting running back, was also out.

The week before, in a 29–0 loss to Syracuse, the Mids managed just 113 yards in total offense. Oh, and Navy fumbled away the first two possessions against the Gamecocks. Nobody, including the Midshipmen, thought the result was possible. "Look at the situation. We're battered and beaten and everyone's hurting and you figure we have no chance at all," Navy quarterback Bob Misch told the *Washington Post*'s Christine Brennan. "South Carolina, on the other hand, is on a roll and heading for the Orange Bowl."

So sure were Gamecocks fans that more than six thousand had already bought tickets. Worse, No. 1 Nebraska fell that day, 17–7, which had left the door open for South Carolina to take over the top slot the next week against Clemson. "Every couple of weeks, someone will bring up the Navy game," former Gamecock lineman Bill Barnhill told Charleston's *Post and Courier* before Navy's visit in 2011. "It was the toughest loss of my life.... You just think about what might have been."

The contingent representing the Orange Bowl stopped in the Navy locker room after the game to congratulate the Midshipmen. "The rumor is that they [the Midshipmen] are high on our list," said Nick Crane, chairman of the bowl's selection committee, to the *Post*.

At 4-5-1, Navy was headed for a 28–11 loss to Army, while South Carolina settled for the Gator Bowl and a 21–14 loss to Oklahoma State. But for one day, Navy turned the college football world upside down. "Your parents always tell you beware of the man who has nothing to lose," former Navy tackle Eric Rutherford told *USA Today* in 2011. "We had nothing to lose that day. We let it all go."

## DECEMBER 7, 1963: NO. 2 NAVY 21, ARMY 15; JANUARY 1, 1964: NO. 1 TEXAS 28, NO. 2 NAVY 6 (COTTON BOWL)

During a span of twenty-five days in 1963, Navy played two of the most difficult games in college football history. The Midshipmen, four points from being ranked No. 1, won the most surreal Army-Navy game in the rivalry's history as the nation mourned the assassination of President John F. Kennedy.

Two days before he was shot and killed in Dallas, Kennedy penned a note to Navy coach Wayne Hardin. Fully aware he'd be sitting on the Cadet side first and Mids' side second, he wrote, "I expect to be sitting on the winning side when the game ends."

The Saturday after Thanksgiving was the traditional slot for the game, but no one felt like playing. "Kennedy was one of us," former Navy captain and Academy superintendent Tom Lynch told ESPN's Richard

Weintraub.[42] Kennedy wasn't an Academy grad, but his encounter with a Japanese destroyer aboard PT-109 on August 1, 1943, made him a U.S. Navy legend. Now slain, it would be his widow, Jackie, who requested Army-Navy be played in his memory. Rescheduled for December 7 but absent the usual pageantry and spirit of rivalry, a moment of silence and a coin flip was all that took place before the game.

No. 2 Navy led, 21–7, before Army rallied in the final minutes. Rollie Stichweh's touchdown and two-point conversion cut Navy's lead to 21–15 with six minutes left. By the time the last minute started to tick away, Army was on Navy's four but didn't have a way to stop the clock.

Stichweh had been granted a handful of stops during the drive when the crowd noise made hearing signals impossible, costing his team valuable time. With eight seconds left and the clock counting down, officials ignored his final request. Confusion reigned over the Cadets' futile and failed attempt to snap the ball, and the clock expired at the goal line. The post-game celebration was subdued, as the Mids presented the Kennedy family the game ball and Hardin accepted the Cotton Bowl invitation.

That set the stage for a massive showdown: No. 1 Texas versus No. 2 Navy. With a shot at the national title, there was also a chance to make amends for a highly controversial 32–28 loss at SMU in October—one that resulted in game officials being suspended for their perceived slights toward Navy.

Kennedy had been thinking about a possible Texas-Navy matchup, too, at a luncheon in Dallas for which he never arrived, writing, "I like the idea of the Navy-Texas game, personally, and I'd like to do what I can to help, except that I know how you folks feel about federal intervention."[43]

Dallas was the target of America's ire for having allowed a beloved president to be gunned down on a city street in broad daylight, making Navy America's sweetheart in the Cotton Bowl. In a pregame interview on national television, Hardin took advantage of a chance to politick for a national championship, saying, "When the challenger meets the champion, and the challenger wins, there's a new champion."[44]

That's as close as Navy got to the crown. Texas quarterback Duke Carlisle threw a pair of touchdowns before running a third score in from nine yards out to make it 21–0 at half. The Longhorns rolled the Mids, 28–6. Three facts were obvious: Navy needed to play a perfect game to win; the emotional toll of a possible national title, plus Kennedy's death—which had sustained them against Army—hurt against the Longhorns; and Texas was better.

Delivering a Cotton Bowl–record twenty-one completions in thirty-one attempts for 228 yards, Staubach had validated his Heisman. Hardin was gracious, knowing that Staubach would return in 1964. "They outhit us from beginning to end," Hardin said. "They did everything a No. 1 team is expected to do—tackled better, blocked better, ran better and passed better. What more can you ask?"[45]

Navy stumbled to a 3-6-1 record the next season, and the day they played with a chance to win the national title on New Year's Day hasn't been repeated over the following fifty-three seasons.

## JANUARY 1, 1955: NO. 5 NAVY 21, NO. 6 OLE MISS 0 (SUGAR BOWL)

It seems inconceivable today, but Navy's acceptance to play in the Sugar Bowl came on the heels of turning down bids to the Orange Bowl the two previous years. But nicknamed "A Team Called Desire" because of its fierce will to win, these Midshipmen drew national attention and convinced Academy officials to accept the bid. The payout was at least $160,000, revenue badly needed to build Navy–Marine Corps Memorial Stadium on Rowe Boulevard.

This was Navy's first bowl team since the 1924 Rose Bowl team, and they were missing three key performers in the aftermath of the 27–20 win over Army needed to secure the bid. Tackle Jim Royer, Bob Craig—Navy's fastest back—and his replacement, Jack Garrow, were all sidelined for the prep work before the game. Running back John Weaver limped through the practices.

But they overran No. 5 Mississippi, to the surprise of USNA Athletic Director Captain C. Elliott Laughlin. "It's the first bowl game and it means so damn much," Laughlin moaned to Coach Eddie Erdelatz. "With the injuries you have, I just don't feel confident."

"Forget it," Erdelatz said. "We're going to win."[46]

The game was over as soon as it started. The Midshipmen took the opening kickoff and drove it right down Ole Miss's throats, going seventy yards in seventeen plays over seven minutes and thirty seconds. Converting a fourth-and-one from their thirty-nine kept the drive alive, Weaver later bolted twenty-four yards to the Rebel three-yard line. Joe Gattuso, who picked up the fourth-and-one, punched it in for the score.

Rarely does a decision in the first five minutes make for a turning point, but quarterback George Welsh believes that's exactly what happened.

"When I got into the huddle, the guys said, 'C'mon, George. We can make it. Let's try it.' So we had Gattuso slant off tackle. I knew Joe would make a yard," Welsh said.[47]

A practice forgone long ago in college and professional football, Welsh's play-calling was noteworthy to *Sports Illustrated*'s Herman Hickman: "Welsh had more imagination in this game than ever before. He completely baffled Mississippi with his mixture of formations, plays and thinking. If he ever lacked poise, the Army game gave it to him—and remember, Col. Blaik, he has another year."[48]

Welsh hit Weaver for an eighteen-yard score in the third quarter, and Gattuso scored for a second time later in the third to make it 21–0. When it was over, the Southeastern Conference champions admitted that they were believers. "It seemed like all 11 men were after you on every play," Mississippi quarterback Eagle Day said. "That 'desire' stuff might sound corny, but [Navy] had it."

## DECEMBER 2, 1950: NAVY 14, NO. 2 ARMY 2

During the later stages of Navy's unforgettable, fourteen-game winning streak over Army from 2002 to 2015, the obligatory question always popped up: "If Army beats Navy, would it be the biggest upset in the rivalry's history?"

No. The greatest upset in the game's long history will always be the Mids' 14–2 win in 1950. Army hadn't lost in three years; Navy had won just seven games in five seasons. But by upsetting Earl "Red" Blaik's best team, Eddie Erdelatz set himself up for greatness at Navy.

Army and Navy each own a point-to period of Camelot-like success. Army roared through the 1940s and 1950s, while Navy rolled through the 1950s and 1960s. The 1950 game, which Army entered on a twenty-eight-game winning streak, was the day Coach Blaik's dynasty intersected with Navy's budding resurgence under Erdelatz.

Winning just five times during the brutal stretch from 1946 to 1949, Erdelatz needed time to restock talent. With just five wins between 1950 and 1951, his first two teams didn't fare much better. They entered his first Army-Navy game as three-touchdown underdogs, but almost immediately, Navy owned the day.

Bob Zastrow, Navy's husky quarterback, first zigged and then zagged from seven yards out for the first touchdown. Later, eluding Army's rush by rolling to his left, he pivoted and fired a thirty-yard strike later to a leaping Jim Baldinger in the end zone. Amid two Cadets fighting to pry the ball from his hands, Baldinger's catch gave the Mids a 14–0 advantage.

Army's Bob Blaik, son to his legendary father, was intercepted five times, part of an astounding eight Army turnovers on the day. The Cadets lost two fumbles and threw three picks in the fourth quarter alone. While Army's machinery self-destructed on offense gaining a paltry 113 yards, the Midshipmen offense dominated, piling up 268.

The loss ended Army's national championship hopes, although the Cadets needed Oklahoma State to knock off No. 1 Oklahoma and end its thirty-game win streak, which didn't happen. When the game ended, an entire Brigade that braved a miserable day at Philadelphia's Municipal Stadium celebrated, as described by the *New York Times*' Allison Danzig: "The 3,700 Midshipmen were in a delirium of happiness over the seeming miracle they beheld, storming down from the stands to raise Coach Erdelatz, Captain [Tom] Bakke and their other heroes to their shoulders."

The winds of change swept over both programs. Navy struggled to a similar 2-6-1 mark the next year but routed Army, 42–7, and wouldn't post another losing record until 1964. Erdelatz led Navy to an overall record of 50-26-8, including appearances in the Sugar and Cotton Bowls.

Meanwhile, Army suffered a massive cheating scandal four months later, and ninety Cadets—including Blaik's son and twenty-two other football players—were permanently separated.

Both coaches were gone by the end of the decade, as Blaik retired after the 1958 season and Erdelatz was unceremoniously dismissed in the spring of 1959. None of the nine games the two coaches faced off in came close to rivaling their first encounter.

# OCTOBER 30, 1926: NAVY 10, MICHIGAN 0

The signature win of the 1926 season occurred on October 30 at Baltimore's Municipal Stadium, a horseshoe-shaped facility with vaulted arches that sat atop a hill on Thirty-Third Street and featured columns like the Acropolis in Athens, Greece.

Coached by the legendary Fielding Yost and boasting a pair of All-Americans in Benny Friedman and Bennie Oosterbaan, Michigan went 28-

2-1 in Yost's final four seasons from 1922 to 1926 (Yost didn't coach the 1924 season) and won the conference in each season.

The Wolverines, who had handed Navy a 54–0 loss in 1925—the worst loss in program history—joined Navy for a pregame meal at Bancroft Hall. Bealle's *Gangway* described Michigan's players as "filled with a belly full of butter"[49] after gorging on rich, unskimmed milk during a pregame meal.

The Wolverines boarded the Washington, Baltimore & Annapolis Electric Rail, a defunct railway that folded in 1935 but whose landmarks are still in use near the Academy today, and rode out to the stadium, where eighty thousand fans assembled, according to the *Baltimore News-American*.

In a scoreless first half, Michigan looked to take the lead, but Friedman's attempted placekick was blocked by Tom Eddy. Later, a drive that landed Michigan on Navy's ten-yard line left the Maize and Blue stymied when a pass from Friedman to Oosterbaan was knocked down by Hamilton in front of the goal line on third down. On fourth down, Oosterbaan was stopped on a short pass play at Navy's two.

Navy went in front on Hamilton's twenty-eight-yard field goal in the third quarter. In the final quarter, Hamilton, a native of Columbus, Ohio, again used the fake-kick formation to throw over the Michigan front to get Navy close, and when Howard Caldwell plunged through the Michigan front to make it 10–0, the Wolverines had surrendered their first touchdown in two years.

It was sweet payback for the Midshipmen and bitter for the Wolverines— their only loss of Yost's final season. At the game's conclusion, the Brigade stormed the field, tore down both goalposts and carried the markers lining each side of the field away in jubilation. This win, along with previous victories over Purdue and Princeton, gave the Midshipmen the national attention they needed to gain the attention of voters and pollsters who would later decide the nation's champion.

An easy romp over West Virginia Wesleyan, 53–7, preceded a gritty 10–7 triumph over Georgetown. A 35–13 win over Loyola College from Baltimore was all that separated Navy from the epic showdown with Army in Chicago. The breathless, 21-all tie with Army left the Midshipmen with a 9-0-1 record and a share of the national crown, but the win over Michigan was the jewel of the season.

# UNFORGETTABLE SEASONS

## 1926: NATIONAL CHAMPIONS

Like many national titles in the pre–Bowl Championship Series/College Playoff era, the 1926 title was unofficially split, as Navy shared the crown with Alabama and Stanford. The Midshipmen were named No. 1 by the board and Hoagland polls, as well as by several prominent sportswriters, and it is the only season during which Navy claimed a national championship.

The season opened with a 17–13 victory over Purdue at the now-demolished Thompson Stadium. "Buckeye" Tom Hamilton rescued the Mids, twice throwing out of a fake kick formation to lead Navy to victory. Connecting first with Delbert Williamson and then Russell "Whitey" Lloyd, Navy sealed the game-winning score in the final minutes.

Close calls were a Navy trademark in 1926. Trailing Colgate 7–6 with just minutes to play, Navy's defense separated the ball from the Raiders' Clark Shaughnessy just inches before the goal line. Lloyd came out of the crash-up with the football and raced ninety-five yards for a touchdown to secure a breathtaking 13–7 win.

The signature win of the season was a ten-point shutout over Coach Fielding Yost's Michigan Wolverines at Baltimore's Municipal Stadium. More than eighty thousand came out to see the Wolverines' Benny Friedman and Benny Oosterbaan, but Navy blocked a field goal and handed Michigan their only loss of Yost's final season.

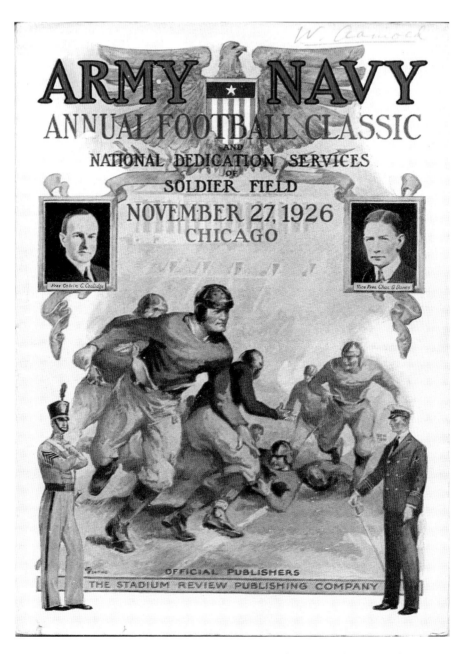

The program cover for the dedication game at Chicago's Soldier Field, the 1926 Army-Navy game. The game ended in a 21-all tie and is considered the mother of all Army-Navy games. *Ron Motl.*

The Mids needed an Alan Shapley interception, a Hamilton touchdown pass to Shapley and a thirty-five-yard Hamilton field goal to escape Georgetown, 10–7, and set up the first memorable battle with Army.

The Army game wasn't played annually until 1930, but with a share of the national title in play for the dedication game for Chicago's new Soldier Field, ticket requests pushed to as high as 600,000 in published reports. Counterfeit tickets swelled the crowd to more than 120,000. After three days of snow and rain, the *Chicago Daily Tribune* declared the battle a toss-up; more than three hundred sportswriters were credentialed for the game.

Navy raced to a 14–0 lead, as Henry Caldwell plowed in from the two on Navy's first possession. After forcing a punt and marching forty-seven yards, Navy's Jim Schuber's touchdown made it 14–0.

But Army buckled down. "Light Horse Harry" Wilson, a transfer from Penn State, plowed across for the Cadets, and when Navy's "Shag" Ransford muffed a punt—it struck his shoulder and bounced off another player's leg and into the end zone—Army's Norris Harbold fell on the ball to tie the game at 14.

In the second half, Harry Wilson and back Chris "Red" Cagle ran wild, with Cagle's forty-three-yard score moving Army in front, 21–14. In the waning moments, Frank Wickhorst, Navy's team captain and All-American tackle, took charge of the Mids' huddle. "Do you guys see that goal line down there?" said Wickhorst, pointing beyond Army's defense with just minutes to play. "We are going to cross it—and we're not going to lose the ball until we put it across."[50]

Facing a fourth and five from the Army's eight with thirty seconds to play, Ingram went for broke, as described in Bealle's *Gangway*:

> *The wingback in motion was Ransford. Hamilton, Shapley and Hannegan were deployed to the right. Army quickly diagnosed the play as a run around their left end and shifted accordingly.…Shapley, unnoticed by any Army player, cut back to the left, went behind Ransford, who deftly slipped the ball into Shapley's hands…running like a frightened deer,* [Shapley] *had a head start around the Army right end and was over for a Navy touchdown. It was a perfectly executed "naked reverse."*

Hamilton's PAT put the game at 21-all, as darkness blanketed Chicago. Undefeated at 9-0-1, Navy's national title share was ensured weeks later when Stanford and Alabama played to a 7–7 tie in the Rose Bowl. It would take thirty-eight years for Navy to return to such a stage, when the No. 2 Midshipmen lost to No. 1 Texas in the 1964 Cotton Bowl, 28–6.

# 1954: 8-2, SUGAR BOWL CHAMPIONS

The confluence of three important accomplishments punctuated 1954, resulting in one of Navy's best seasons and leading to the groundbreaking for its future.

Under George Welsh's steady hand at quarterback, the Mids finished the season ranked No. 5 and won their last four games in convincing fashion, the only close call being when they edged Army, 27–20. By defeating their archrivals for the fourth time in five years, Coach Eddie Erdelatz officially passed Earl Blaik's Cadets, which is exactly what Navy sought when it hired him in 1950.

In the Sugar Bowl, Navy's first bowl game since the 1924 Rose Bowl, the Mids pounced on Mississippi, 21–0. The 8-2 campaign was the most successful since the national title season of 1926 and came as fundraising for the construction of Navy–Marine Corps Memorial Stadium was badly needed, adding significant juice to that effort.

The roots of this success were planted when Navy called "no joy" after four abysmal seasons and handed Erdelatz the helm in 1950. Erdelatz upset Blaik's best team in his first season, but Navy was just 5-12-1 between 1950 and 1951. As Erdelatz stockpiled better talent in the post–World War II era, Navy went 10-5-3 the next two seasons before breaking out in 1954.

Highlights of the season included a 25–0 pasting of Stanford—a victory that earned the Mids their "Team Named Desire" nickname—a 40–7 win over then ACC football power Duke and the victories over Army and Ole Miss at Tulane Stadium on New Year's Day in 1955.

At Stanford, Navy handed the ball to eleven different backs, who shared forty-nine carries. Joe Gattuso ran fourteen times for 153 yards, and Dick Echard was nine for seventeen for two touchdowns in front of more than fifty thousand in Palo Alto, California. "Navy was the best team out there today," Stanford coach Chuck Taylor told the *Stanford Daily*. "They were inspired, we weren't and therefore, they took us apart."

Two missed PATs stymied the Mids in a 21–19 loss at Pittsburgh, and Bob Craig's lost fumble the instant before he crossed the goal line was the difference in a 6–0 loss to Notre Dame in Baltimore. But Welsh found his groove as a signal-caller, and Navy rolled the rest of the season.

Gattuso scored two touchdowns and racked up 111 yards in the Sugar Bowl, winning Most Valuable Player, while John Weaver went for 106 yards and hauled in a touchdown pass from Welsh. Running the "Navy T" option offense, Welsh was eight for fourteen for 76 yards and "was a genius at calling plays today," according to Erdelatz. "Shutting out Mississippi, 21–0, in the Sugar Bowl really spoke volumes about how good we were," Welsh said. "I shared the quarterbacking duties for a couple months, but Weaver was bigger and stronger than me and moved to halfback. That made a big difference."

It seems quaint today, almost comical, but according to Welsh, the real treat of the season was being able to *stay* a few extra nights in the dorms at the University of Tulane after whitewashing Ole Miss. "No one gave it a second thought, staying at the dormitory. You couldn't pull that off today," Welsh said. "After the game, we were able to stay two more nights—they had a dance for us the night after the game—and that's what made it worth it."

## 1957: 9-1-1, COTTON BOWL CHAMPIONS

With a complicated stadium issue dominating Navy's off-field agenda and a burgeoning national civil rights movement seeping into the Academy's football program, Navy's outstanding 1957 season was a welcome respite. Meanwhile, a number of storm fronts were approaching the program from afar. Redeeming what was lost in a bitter tie against Army the year before, Navy marched to the first nine-win season since the national title season of 1926 and won their first ever appearance in the Cotton Bowl.

Poised to play in the Cotton Bowl, a frustrating 7–7 tie with Army in 1956 prompted Rear Admiral William R. Smedburg III to declare, "If you're not good enough to beat Army, then you're not good enough to play in the Cotton Bowl."

There would be no such heartbreak in 1957. The Mids blanked Coach Earl Blaik's Cadets, 14–0, and then marched into Dallas and walked over Rice, 20–7. With two major bowl wins in four seasons, fundraising had Navy on the cusp of opening the Navy–Marine Corps Stadium.

But things were changing while enthusiasm soared; the Cotton Bowl victory was the apex of the Erdelatz era. Navy went 6-3 in 1958, but unable to figure out Army's "Lonesome End" scheme, Blaik beat Erdelatz, who had worn out his welcome in Annapolis; he was fired in the spring of 1959.

The only blemish of 1957 was a 13–7 loss at North Carolina. A 6–6 tie at Duke kept Navy from their first ten-win season in fifty-two years, but the notable victories included a 21–6 win at California, a 27–14 win over

Georgia and the Mids' first back-to-back wins over Notre Dame since the 1933–34 seasons.

Social justice was beginning to make headlines and seeped into Navy's football program, too. The Georgia game was originally scheduled for Baltimore but was moved to Athens, Georgia, in hopes of attracting a bigger gate. But Georgia refused to guarantee nonsegregated seating, and that's how the game ended up in Norfolk, Virginia's forty-seven-thousand-seat Oyster Bowl.

The stadium issue was also of big concern. Navy was traveling to Washington, Baltimore, Philadelphia and Norfolk regularly to host home games; twelve-thousand-seat Thompson Stadium was no longer a suitable site to host regular season games. Bickering between Academy leadership in Annapolis and the secretary of the navy in D.C. about commissioning the project, as well as how big it would be and how to pay for the site in the Admiral Heights section of Annapolis that borders Rowe Boulevard, dominated the program's buzz off the field.

But the Cotton Bowl showcased Navy's balance and depth. Tom Forrestal, who racked up 153 yards passing, and Joe Tranchini, who scored on a 1-yard keeper, split the quarterbacking duties. Ned Oldham and Harry Hurst each had more than 50 yards rushing and both scored, while Tony Stremic and Maxwell Award winner Bob Reifsnyder dominated the offensive line and were primarily responsible for Navy's 375 yards of offense.

## 2016: 9-5

An enchanting season, Navy reached the doorstep of one of the most successful years in program history and then saw that door slam in its face in heartbreaking fashion. Poised to snatch a Cotton Bowl bid from undefeated Western Michigan, three straight losses ended 2016 with a resounding *thud*.

Navy replaced thirty-six seniors, including program legend Keenan Reynolds and ten other starters, only to lose starting quarterback Tago Smith in the second quarter of the season opener. The Midshipmen suffered more injuries than any FBS school. But Will Worth, previously a third-string quarterback and placeholder, became a household name who led the nation in rushing touchdowns and set the single-season record for total yards with 2,595.

The dramatic and unexplainable quickly became Navy's trademark. The Midshipmen were winning, often running away, when trends and statistics ordinarily defy victory. In twelve of Navy's fourteen games, the Mids' defense gave up the opening score.

After blowing a 21–0 lead, Navy needed a last-minute touchdown and goal line stand to defeat Connecticut, 28–24. At the one-yard line, the Huskies, who inexplicably called a running play with no timeouts, couldn't get another play off after the Mids buried Ron Johnson inches from the goal line on the game's final play.

They entered the Air Force game 3-0 but dropped a listless, 28–14 decision and lost co-captain and linebacker Daniel Gonzales for the season to a Lisfranc fracture. With both captains—and likely the Commander-in-Chief Trophy—lost and No. 6 Houston up next, the season could have crumbled. Instead, Navy stunned the nation with the biggest upset of the season over the undefeated Cougars, 46–40, in Annapolis. It was Navy's first win over a Top 10 team in thirty-two years.

They surrendered a one-hundred-yard kickoff return and Worth fumbled at the pylon, but a four-play, goal line stand and a fumble recovery with 3:39 to play saved a 42–28 win over Memphis.

In November, Navy punted just twice. A breathtaking 28–27 win over Notre Dame saw the Midshipmen limit the Fighting Irish to just six possessions—the Mids didn't punt—to defeat Notre Dame for the fourth time in the last ten years.

Ranked No. 18, Navy hosted Temple in the AAC title game but watched helplessly as its conference title and New Year's Day bowl aspirations were systematically dismantled. Already down, 21–0, Worth and slotback Toney Gulley were lost for the season. Later, backs Dishan Romine and Darryl Bonner and wideout Tyler Carmona were also injured, and a 34–10 loss snapped a fifteen-game home winning streak.

Averaging almost fifty-three points and 537 yards in the final six AAC games was suddenly a distant memory, as injuries exposed Navy's lack of depth when it mattered most. Freshman Zach Abey was forced to make his first career start at quarterback against Army—the first time in program history that happened—and he was predictably outplayed before his spectacular, forty-one-yard run put Navy ahead, 17–14, with 12:42 left. But the Mids couldn't hold the lead—or retake it—and Army ended fourteen years of futility with a 21–17 win. Almost two thousand Cadets poured over the rails and onto the turf in Baltimore in celebration.

In the Armed Forces Bowl, Louisiana Tech survived the depleted Midshipmen, 52–45.

The ride was over, but its improbability and exhilaration was committed to memory—appropriate solace for a season that bordered on the cusp of greatness and ended in despair.

# G.O.A.T.S.

## PLAYERS

## NO. 80: RON BEAGLE, TE, 1953–55

His numbers weren't gaudy, but his accomplishments were undeniable and he opened a pathway to Annapolis for another Navy legend in Roger Staubach. Ron Beagle was a sixty-minute-per-game performer, a key requirement under Coach Eddie Erdelatz in the early 1950s, when Navy didn't enjoy the same depth their opponents did. He was a two-way performer who blocked, tackled, received the football and ran after the catch with equal precision.

A First Team All-American in back-to-back seasons (1954–55) despite a lithe six-foot-one, 185-pound build, his determined approach to the game fit with Navy's 1954 "Team Named Desire" that pounded Ole Miss in the Sugar Bowl, 21–0. That season, Navy finished 8-2 with the No. 5 ranking.

Beagle won the Maxwell Award—the first of four Navy players to win college football's player of the year award—and was nominated for the Heisman Trophy after catching thirty passes and 451 yards and four touchdowns.

For his career, Beagle hauled in sixty-four passes, most often thrown by fellow Navy legend George Welsh, and racked up 849 yards and eight touchdowns. This is remarkable because like today's era of success at Navy, the Mids primarily ran the ball; passing plays were called at a premium. "Off the field, [Beagle] was quiet and reserved, a complete contrast to how he played....He was thoroughly aggressive for his size, and he had tremendous hands," Welsh said.[51]

His tenacity, speed and skill made him a natural for lacrosse, too, where he was a two-time All-American and earned another three letters.

Good enough to be drafted by the Chicago Cardinals in the seventeenth round of the 1956 NFL Draft, Beagle instead completed his four-year tour of duty in the Marine Corps. His football days behind him, Beagle relocated to Sacramento, California, where he died in 2015.

Born in Hartford, Connecticut, Beagle played at Purcell High School in Cincinnati, where Roger Staubach starred before becoming a college and pro football icon.

Beagle was inducted into the College Football Hall of Fame in 1986.

## NO. 58: BOB REIFSNYDER, T, 1956–58

In Navy's "Camelot" era, a period remarkable for Navy's on-field success and the outstanding talent who made it possible, it would be impossible to overlook Bob Reifsnyder.

Known as "Reif" to coaches and teammates, he terrorized the opposing line of scrimmage so much that he was named the Maxwell Award winner—Navy's second national player of the year winner in four seasons—and earned First Team All-American honors in 1957. That Navy team went 9-1-1, won the Lambert Trophy as the best team in the East and walked all over Rice in the Cotton Bowl, 20–7.

"'Reif' was a dominating player in his time and could have starred at Notre Dame just as easily," said Steve Belichick, an assistant coach under Eddie Erdelatz and father to Bill Belichick. "He was a terrific fullback in high school, but the first time he showed up for practice and Erdelatz saw this big, brawny kid standing 6-foot-2 and weighing 240 [pounds], he said, 'We can't afford the luxury of a guy that big in the backfield. Put him on the line.'"[52]

During the fourth quarter of 1957's 14–0 win over Army, Reifsnyder and Army tackle Bill Melnick became entangled, and Reifsnyder lost one of his teeth. "When I went after him, the referee, who happened to be Albie Booth, the great player from Yale, threw us both out," Reifsnyder told the Baltimore Sun's Alan Goldstein in 1997. "[Albie] acted as if he felt sorry for me."

Coming out of New York's Baldwin High School near the Long Island Sound, Iowa and Maryland had eyes on Reifsnyder. Being recruited by former Heisman Trophy winner Doc Blanchard, Reifsnyder was smitten with Army, but that changed during a visit to Annapolis with Erdelatz. "Annapolis and the white dress uniforms were easier on the eyes," Reifsnyder said.[53]

His playing days, as well as his military career, ended in 1958 due to an Achilles' heel injury so severe that he appeared in just one game, a cameo appearance in the season's Army game. He graduated from the Academy but didn't receive a commission; he was granted an honorable discharge from further military service.

Holding a degree without a career to ply, Reifsnyder tried professional football after being drafted by the Los Angeles Rams in the fourth round in 1959. But the injury had zapped Reif of the quickness that made him such a devastating factor in 1957, and he was cut. Another failed tryout with the Los Angeles Chargers followed before he latched on with the New York Titans.

Reifsnyder made $13,000—major money for the day—but the team and the league was at best a minor-league experience. "I could write a book about my times with the Titans," Reifsnyder said, laughing. "They were a real rag-tag outfit run by the old broadcaster, Harry Wismer....The league was pretty bush."[54]

Those who can no longer play teach, and Reifsnyder was adept at that, too. He coached football at Berner High School in Massapequa, New York, from 1963 to 1980, going 104-39-3. He was an assistant at Columbia University from 1981 to 1984 and bounced between three high schools and academies for the remainder of his coaching career.

His son, Bob Jr., followed his father to Annapolis, played Sprint football and became a Navy pilot.

Reifsnyder was inducted into the College Football Hall of Fame in 1997.

## NO. 27: JOE BELLINO, HB, 1958–60

He wasn't the greatest running back in Naval Academy history. He didn't have blazing "Point A to Point B" speed, either. What Joe Bellino did possess, though, was the strength of a Clydesdale and the lightning-quick first step and the determination of Secretariat, a combination that made Bellino a brilliantly gifted workhorse.

With massive calves and stump-like thighs, Joe Bellino's first step was almost as powerful as his determined approach to the game. *University of Maryland/Hornbake Library.*

His calves were so legendary that the elastic ribbon at the top of the sock cut off circulation to his feet. New, shorter socks were ordered following the 1959 opener at Boston College. In that game, Bellino scored a fifty-yard touchdown in a 24–8 win, and it was a precursor to his ability to generate speed, break tackles and outrun his opponents for the next two years.

In the 1959 Maryland game, his fifty-nine-yard punt return with six minutes left was the difference in a 22–14 win in Baltimore. Later that season, Bellino terrorized the Cadets for three touchdowns as Navy romped past Army, 43–12.

In 1960, his three touchdowns and an interception were part of Navy's first game with Air Force, a 35–3 romp. Bellino had an impressive four-touchdown effort in a 41–6 win over Virginia—the first Midshipman to accomplish such a feat—but it was his interception that saved the Mids' 17–12 win over Army.

After the game, an excited Navy publicist raced up to Bellino and proclaimed, "That play just won you the Heisman Trophy!" Bellino responded, "Who are you kidding? That play saved me from being a goat." He would later explain to a reporter, "I had fumbled at the 30 and they were going in for the winning touchdown."[55]

Clinching a berth in the Orange Bowl led Bellino, one of the last two-way players, to Navy's first Heisman Trophy.

Bellino took 436 first-place votes and earned 1,793 overall points, outpacing UCLA's Billy Kilmer, Pittsburgh's Mike Ditka and Ohio State's Tom Matte. Bellino also collected the Maxwell Award and was a unanimous selection for All-American at halfback. Despite a loss to Missouri in Miami, the Mids (9-2) finished No. 4 in the country in the Associated Press poll.

Unlike today, plebes (called freshmen at civilian schools) didn't play. In three years of varsity competition, Bellino racked up thirty-one touchdowns, ran for 1,664 yards, piled up 833 yards in kick returns and began his military career owning fifteen Academy records.

Bellino was also an accomplished baseball player, catching and playing the outfield while hitting .428 in 1959 and .320 in 1960 and captaining the 1961 Midshipmen.

The Academy retired Bellino's number, 27, before the Orange Bowl in 1960, and after he completed his four-year service stint, he played three years with the Boston Patriots. During this time, Bellino remained in the U.S. Navy reserves and ultimately earned a captain rank.

Bellino was inducted into the College Football Hall of Fame in 1977.

## NO. 51: TOM LYNCH, C/LB, 1961–63

Bill Belichick describes Tom Lynch as the prototypical football captain. Lynch's dossier is littered with stories of exceptional leadership, but more than anything, he knew how to frame the day-to-day grind of football to get the most out of his teammates.

My favorite example was detailed in Jack Clary's *Navy Football: Gridiron Legends and Fighting Heroes*. The 1963 Midshipmen, Navy's greatest team in program history, had taken down Michigan, 26–13, before hammering No. 3 and undefeated Pittsburgh, 24–12.

Now the Mids found themselves tied at 7 at halftime in their usual dogfight at Notre Dame. Lynch ordered Navy's best player, Roger Staubach, out of the locker room before admonishing his teammates that further lackluster play would jeopardize Staubach's legitimate Heisman Trophy possibilities.

The message? When Staubach achieves greatness, so does the team, so his success was their success. Lynch wasn't the *most* talented player—that was Staubach—but he was the most talented leader, and it showed that day in a locker room in South Bend, Indiana.

Converting an individual award into a team mission was a brilliant directive, and his highly unusual method resulted in Navy marching for three quick touchdowns in the third quarter. With a 35–14 win in the books, the Midshipmen went on to pummel Maryland and Duke before winning the most emotional Army-Navy game in the rivalry's history, 21–15.

The Midshipmen played Texas for the national title in the Cotton Bowl and lost, 28–6, ending the season with the No. 2 ranking. "All of my captains [at Navy] were elected by their teammates," Coach Wayne Hardin said in February 2017. "Of that group, Tom Lynch was a slam-dunk of a choice."

Akin to a catcher in baseball, Lynch was Navy's unofficial field general, identifying formations and calling coverage assignments. But his contributions to Navy football didn't end when he took his pads off. He was superintendent at the Academy from 1991 to 1994 and was part of the search committee during the pivotal moment in Navy's football renaissance: the hiring of Paul Johnson. "I remember saying to Paul, 'Coach, the track record of guys coming from Division II and I-AA to Division-I hasn't been that great,'" Lynch said. "Paul said, 'Look at the schools they get selected for, too.' He named a few, and that showed me he was the guy to bring the Navy football program around. He's a big reason it is what it is today."

To this day, Lynch oozes affinity for the method and mission of the Academy. "You can talk X's and O's—how difficult is that?—but a coach has to believe in the purpose and the mission of the institution," Lynch said. "The Naval Academy requires 140 credit hours in four years, 90 which come from math, science and engineering. You're a Midshipman first and a football player second."

## NO. 12: ROGER STAUBACH, QB, 1962–64

Spanning 136 seasons, players like Roger Staubach and Joe Bellino and the Army-Navy game are stanchions of the program in Annapolis, but Navy football is so much more, and that overarching premise is what motivated this title.

But there's never been a player like Staubach—as evidenced by the hundreds of books, magazine and newspaper articles dedicated to Staubach's exploits on and off the field. He remains iconic, and wherever the Midshipmen play, Staubach's appearance simultaneously surprises no one at Navy while causing a buzz. Tweets and posts announcing, "Roger is here!" overwhelm Twitter and Facebook when No. 12 is in the house.

As self-effacing as any Midshipman when it came to his immense talents, he was a regular attendee of Mass, struggled to reach a 3.0 grade point average because of mechanical drawing and metallurgy and, like other students, earned demerits. But his football acumen was an unmatched dynamic, and his classmates within the Brigade knew it, often asking for his autograph on "The Yard."

His play evoked many nicknames, like "Roger the Dodger" and "Captain America," and drew heady comparisons. He scrambled like Fran Tarkington, threw like Johnny Unitas and was a weapon unlike any other until Keenan Reynolds rewrote the record book more than fifty years after Staubach played his final game as a Midshipman. "More people would like to see Roger Staubach right now than any celebrity," Hardin told a national magazine during the 1963 season. "If we opened the doors, do you have any idea how many writers and photographers would show up at our practices? A dozen? It would be closer to 5,000."[56]

Staubach was the headliner when No. 2 Navy reached the Cotton Bowl against No. 1 Texas to decide the 1963 championship. Navy lost, 28–6, but Coach Wayne Hardin remembered the toughness his quarterback exhibited when the deck was stacked against him. "As a football player, Staubach was a true soldier in a sailor's world," Hardin said in his final interview before passing away on April 12, 2017. "He was a pressure player who could deliver when it mattered most. People remember the great wins we had in 1963, but I remember the SMU game we lost. Roger was getting killed—I think he came out twice because of injury—but at the very end, he still threw the pass that should have won the game. Skippy [Orr] dropped it, but the only reason we had a chance to win was Roger."

Beyond Navy, he served four years in Vietnam, where the lessons learned in 1964—a frustrating 3-6-1 senior season—served him well. Going back to football for the Dallas Cowboys in 1969, Staubach was the most notable player on "America's Team" as the league was evolving into the multibillion-dollar enterprise it is today. Over eleven seasons, "Captain Comeback" led twenty-three game-winning drives.

His playing career ended in 1979—the Pro Hall of Fame called in 1985—and Staubach entered the private sector and became a captain of industry, too.

Staubach's legendary playing exploits have faded, while his compassion and willingness to help friends and former teammates remains omnipresent. His goodwill ushered success for so many when they needed it most. And whenever Navy calls, Staubach answers. "He was the face of the program when we were great and when we fell on hard times, too, and he's been an ambassador for our rise the last two decades," Naval Academy Athletic Director Chet Gladchuk said. "Every program should be so lucky to have someone like Roger Staubach in their history. We've just been incredibly blessed to have the one and only real deal."

Staubach was inducted into the College Football Hall of Fame in 1981.

# NO. 48: CHET MOELLER, DB, 1973–75

One of the best defensive backs to ever play at Navy, Chet Moeller played the run so well in his last two seasons (1974–75) that teams purposefully ran away from his side of the field. That prompted Coach George Welsh to move him into a rover position to keep opposing offenses uncertain where Moeller would line up from play to play.

Len Fontes, appointed by Welsh as Moeller's position coach, was the difference maker in Moeller's career. Fontes pushed Moeller, a sophomore from Ohio who struggled to get snaps, to use film from practice and games as an instrument of improvement. The change in results was dramatic. From hardly used reserve to second team by the end of his sophomore year, Moeller was named a starter by his junior season. "I never lost the position and started every game from that point on," Moeller told Tommy Hicks of the *Press-Register* in 2011.

In 1974, Navy upset Penn State in a monsoon, 7–6. The Mids forced Penn State into five fumbles, one of which Moeller recovered. But the real storm was No. 48. He made an astounding thirteen tackles. Three of those tackles were for loss—part of twenty-five he made behind the line of scrimmage that season—a total that remains Navy's season record.

As a senior in 1975, Moeller was East Coast Athletic Conference Player of the Year and was a force to be reckoned with on a Navy defense that was ranked third nationally. His interception against Syracuse set up a score in a 10–6 win over the Orangemen in Annapolis. When the Mids shut out Pitt,

17–0, it was Moeller who hauled down eventual Heisman Trophy winner Tony Dorsett at the goal line. He later recovered a fumble to trigger Navy's first scoring drive, and his fifty-four-yard interception return set up a field goal.

Named an Associated Press Player of the Week during that season, Moeller was invited to the Coaches' All-America game, where he received the Ernie Davis Award.

Moeller co-captained a Navy team that posted the program's first winning season (7-4) since 1967 and won the Commander-in-Chief Trophy outright for the second time in three years. Nationally, media and coaches recognized him as a game-changer. He was named a unanimous First Team All-American—just the sixth Midshipmen to earn such an honor—and a Second Team Academic All-American, too.

Moeller left Navy as a two-time ECAC All-Conference honoree with 275 career tackles, an astounding total for a defensive back or safety. He served as an officer in the Marine Corps and was inducted into the College Football Hall of Fame in 2002.

# NO. 40: EDDIE MEYERS, RB, 1979–81

His nickname was "Fast Eddie," but Eddie Meyers was a workhorse in an era of Navy football when the best players did everything. And Eddie Meyers was willing to do anything to help his team win. Run the football? Oh, yeah. Meyers did a lot of that. Catch passes out of the backfield? He did that, too. Return kicks? Meyers was on it, and his teams won a lot because of it—the Mids went 31-15-1 and played in three bowl games during Meyers's four years.

He was even voted the Most Valuable Player in the 1981 Liberty Bowl, a game Navy *lost* to No. 15 Ohio State, 31–28. "We spotted them 14 points before we decided we could play on the same field with those guys," Meyers said.

After fighting his way into the lineup from the seventh string as a sophomore, he rushed for 279 yards on forty-two carries against Army and finished his Academy career with 2,935 rushing yards.

As a senior, Meyers ran for 298 yards and scored four touchdowns against Syracuse; his 331 all-purpose yards in that game remains a Navy record against a Division I opponent. He was a 1981 Honorable Mention All-American and was named the College Football Player of the Year by the now-defunct Downtown Athletic Club in New York City.

Along the way, Meyers paved the way for another legend to follow his footsteps: Napoleon McCallum. "Football was something you did," Meyers said of his Academy career. "You weren't expected to play in the pros. You were expected to go in the Navy."

But "Fast Eddie" did both, taking his leave time to play with the Atlanta Falcons during his six-year stretch of service. During his time as a supply officer at Camp Pendleton, he spent leave at the Falcons' training camp. When he was finally discharged, he made the Falcons' roster in 1987, only to suffer a career-ending, turf-toe injury.

As he watches more Navy players, in addition to players from other service academies, chase their NFL dreams, there's a part of him that sours on his NFL experience. "We should have been allowed to do more—Phil McConkey, and Napoleon and I—to be even considered to play in the NFL," Meyers said. "I get more respect from former NFL players when they find out I was National Player of the Year at Navy than I ever did from the Academy."

Still, his name is notable within the Navy record book. Most rushing attempts in a game, Meyers is second (43) and tied twice for third (42), and he's fifth all-time in a season (277). His eight 100-yard rushing games in a season was the best ever until he was joined by McCallum, Keenan Reynolds and Will Worth, and his fourteen career 100-yard games is still tied as a program-best mark.

Meyers was the first Midshipman to rush for 200 yards in a game, something he did twice, and his 279 yards rushing is still the Army-Navy game record. "Every time I go see Army-Navy, I think, 'This is the year they'll break that record,'" Meyers told the *Baltimore Sun* in 2015. "But it has held up."[57]

## NO. 80: PHIL MCCONKEY, WR, 1976–78

At just five-foot-ten and 160 pounds, Phil McConkey's biggest assets were his heart and will to win. "The competitiveness never goes away," McConkey told the *Baltimore Sun* in 2015. "I grew up with an enormous chip on my shoulder because, at every level, I was told I was too small to play football. I had something to prove so on every play, I went full throttle."

Recruited as "that skinny little kid from Buffalo,"[58] McConkey was a star on a Navy team that played a powerhouse schedule in 1978 and led the Midshipmen to their first nine-win season and bowl appearance in fifteen years.

His name remains a mainstay within the Navy record books. Most punt returns in a game? That's McConkey (seven), and most in a career (eighty), too. He's tied for first in touchdown receptions in a season (six) and a career (thirteen), and his 1,278 receiving yards are second only to Rob Taylor (1,736).

But it was his performance in the 1978 Holiday Bowl that Annapolitians and Navy fans remember most. The Mids were in danger of being blown out against BYU, trailing 16–3 early in the second half. McConkey's sixteen-yard run on a reverse out of the backfield triggered a seventy-seven-yard touchdown drive to get Navy back in the game. In the fourth quarter, McConkey's sixty-five-yard touchdown from Bob Lesczcynski put Navy in front to stay, and he was named the Most Valuable Player of a 23–16 win.

For the next five years, McConkey saw more dangerous action, trading his football uniform for a flight suit, and the only play calls he heard was intercom chatter as a helicopter pilot transporting nuclear weapons.

Discharged at twenty-seven, McConkey signed with the New York Giants at an age when most players retire from the NFL; the average professional career lasts less than four years. But waiting six years made McConkey's hunger growl louder to prove himself all over again.

McConkey appeared in thirteen games in 1984, primarily as a kickoff and punt returner, for Coach Bill Parcells. He was consistently in the league's top ten for punt and kickoff return yardage during his six-year career that spanned eighty-four games. That he appeared in all sixteen regular season games in 1985 and 1986 was a testament to his ability to withstand the physical toll of the NFL.

A role player for his first three seasons, McConkey picked the most opportune time—Super Bowl XXI—to show a worldwide audience what people in Annapolis already knew: he was a gamer when it mattered most. His twenty-five-yard punt return led to a Giants' field goal, and a forty-four-yard reception set up a touchdown. Later, he snatched a deflected pass from six yards out for a touchdown of his own as New York romped past Denver, 39–20. "Everyone talks what Roger Staubach did—deservedly so, too—but what Phil did was even more incredible because Phil was a pilot," said former Navy great Eddie Meyers, who followed McConkey to the NFL in 1987. "It took him six years before he even got on an NFL field, and he played....He did a hell of a job in the Super Bowl."

# NO. 30: NAPOLEON MCCALLUM, RB, 1981–85

What he wanted to do more than anything was run in the National Football League. In the end, he convinced the NFL to run toward him. Napoleon McCallum will always be the greatest Navy player ever who didn't win the Heisman Trophy, and his remarkable career recalls some of the unique things that *didn't* happen for McCallum, arguably the greatest back the Mids ever suited up.

McCallum was a favorite for the Heisman in 1984 after leading the nation in 1983 with 2,395 all-purpose yards—rushing, receiving and kick returns—a performance so dominant for a 3-8 team he finished sixth in the Heisman balloting.

All of it prompted the Academy to unabashedly generate an "I Have Not Begun to Run" campaign, a John Paul Jones reference, in advance of his senior year, but the campaign slogan ended up being true for the wrong reasons. McCallum broke his left leg against Virginia in the second game of 1984.

Without Coach Gary Tranquill's "Big Guy," Navy limped to a 3-8 mark, their only Division I win a shocking 38–21 victory over no. 2 South Carolina that kept the Gamecocks from playing for the national title in the Orange Bowl.

Motivated by the unfortunate circumstances, Navy offered McCallum something previously offered to no other player: a fifth year of eligibility. But the momentum from 1983 never transferred to his second-chance season in 1985.

Still, McCallum set twenty-three program records, and his farewell game included forty-one carries and 219 yards rushing against Army—more than all the Cadets combined—in a 17–7 win. The Mids carried him off the field.

McCallum's number, 30, was retired after the season, and the Oakland Raiders selected him in the fourth round of that spring's draft. Realizing that they were looking at a once-in-a-generation type of talent, the U.S. Navy afforded McCallum weekend liberty to play for the Raiders while serving on the USS *Peleliu*, an amphibious helicopter carrier docked in Long Beach, California. It was the first time the Navy made such a concession. He delivered 536 yards rushing, but the U.S. Navy rescinded the order, and McCallum was transferred to a war ship on the Indian Ocean the following season and didn't return to pro football until 1990.

McCallum returned to the Raiders after discharge and lasted until opening night of the 1994 season. Wrestled down by San Francisco's Ken Norton Jr. in the third quarter, McCallum's knee bent backward at a gruesome angle. While dislocating his knee, he'd torn three ligaments and shredded his hamstring and calf off the bone. Six surgeries, including repair of artery and nerve damage, meant that McCallum would never play again.

Some of his records have fallen, but the single-season rushing record of 1,587 yards—a mark Reynolds missed by 214—and career all-purpose yards record of 7,172 will likely stand forever. "I know I was trained as a naval officer," McCallum told the *Los Angeles Times* in 2010. "But [Navy] spends so much in recruiting, I thought we'd have gotten more bang for our buck if I'd been used in that way. Every time I stepped on the field, you'd have heard something about the Navy."

But at the same time, there's no bitterness toward Navy—or the way his career ended. "I'm thankful because I did play and I beat the odds," McCallum told the *Times*. "Most NFL running backs last, like, two years, and I got six."

McCallum, employed by the Las Vegas Sands Corporation and friends with Oakland Raiders owner Mark Davis, finally got his due for his idea for the Raiders to relocate to Las Vegas that dated back to 2015, according to Chase Whittemore of Argentum Partners—the lobbying team that successfully pushed through $750 million in public funding for the Raiders stadium via the Nevada state legislature, according to the *Reno Gazette-Journal*.

McCallum was inducted into the College Football Hall of Fame in 2002.

# NO. 51: CLINT BRUCE, LB, 1993–96

As accomplished as Clint Bruce was on the field, it will always pale in comparison to his military and post-military career. A four-time letterman, Bruce ended his Navy career with 328 tackles, fifth best in program history. He led the team in tackles in 1995–96 (117, 125) and captained the 1996 Midshipmen, who went 9-3 and captured a come-from-behind 41–38 win over California in the Aloha Bowl. It was the program's first bowl victory in eighteen seasons, and Bruce was named Most Valuable Player by the Annapolis Touchdown Club.

After suffering through a combined 7-15 record in his first two years, Bruce was a primary player in Navy's 14-9 record his final two years. "I had a deep animosity for anyone who didn't wear the same color helmet as I did, so winning the way we did as a senior, ruining Air Force's homecoming and winning the Aloha Bowl, was extremely satisfying," Bruce said. "There were former players saying we should drop down to I-AA, so after the losing and uncertainty, the enthusiasm around the program was awesome."

Bruce tried out with the Baltimore Ravens (1997) and New Orleans Saints (1999), and during tryouts, he completed SEAL training and reporting to SEAL Team V and then went on to complete BUDS (Basic Underwater Demolition SEAL) training in 1998 with Class 217.

He didn't make it to professional football, but his mission to succeed didn't stop. During Hurricane Katrina, Bruce was part of a group that successfully rescued more than seven hundred people from New Orleans's Fairmont Hotel. Bruce co-founded Trident Response Group (TRG) in 2005, now a multi-office managing risk for America's best leaders, businesses and families.

A handful of years later, driven to honor fallen military, police and firefighters, Bruce advocated for "Memorial May" to better the effort of Memorial Day and founded Carry the Load (CTL). Since 2011, CTL has awarded more than $3 million to nonprofits serving military and first responders.

Finally, Bruce founded Hold Fast in 2012, a conduit to creating "after military life chapters" for veterans on the professional speaker and life coach circuits. Bruce was awarded the Marine Military Academy's Iwo Jima Leadership Award for post-military leadership and the America's Future Series' Megellas Award for post-military community impact. More recently, Bruce received the University of Texas–Dallas's Center for Brain Health Legacy Award for contributions to its groundbreaking research and impact on traumatic brain injury and posttraumatic stress.

## NO. 19: KEENAN REYNOLDS, QB, 2012–15

He made his debut against Air Force as an unknown, untested plebe, led an improbable comeback and spent the next four years rewriting Navy's record books. That's the alpha and omega of the legend of Keenan Reynolds, the rare player who was worthy of a scholarship from a Power 5 school and fell into Navy's lap instead.

"We looked at recruiting Keenan, too, at Georgia Tech," Yellow Jackets coach Paul Johnson said. "But we took the high school player of the year in North Carolina instead. We missed…a lot of other schools missed on Keenan. He was a great, great football player."

Reynolds was thrust into Navy's football vernacular on October 6, 2012, when he replaced Trey Miller with ten minutes to play in the fourth quarter at Air Force. The Mids were down, 21–13, and Reynolds marched the Blue and Gold down the field and into the end zone before Noah Copeland scored the two-point conversion to tie the game.

Navy outlasted the Falcons in overtime, 28–21, and the next week, Ken Niumatalolo handed Reynolds the reins on a Friday night in Mt. Pleasant, Michigan. Reynolds threw three touchdowns; Navy rolled Central Michigan, 31–13; and Niumatalolo never looked back. "Keenan played so well," Niumatalolo said. "Trey knew it would be tough to get his spot back."

For the next four years, Reynolds surpassed almost everyone in the Navy record books. The national attention started in 2015, when Reynolds began knocking down NCAA records.

By some counts, up to five hundred people specifically came to see Reynolds on November 7, 2015, at the Liberty Bowl. Navy manhandled No. 13 and previously undefeated Memphis, 45–20, on national television, eliminating the primary hurdle between the Mids and a showdown in Houston for a berth in the first American Athletic Conference title game.

Seeing Reynolds set the FBS record for rushing touchdowns in a career was a possibility, too. He had started the game with seventy-seven, tied with Wisconsin's Montee Ball. With the record one yard away, what happened next was so "Keenan," described perfectly by *Sports Illustrated*'s Ben Reiter:

> *When Reynolds approached the line, though, he saw that his coaches' plans would come as no surprise to Memphis. Nine Tigers were in the box, and every gap was plugged....Reynolds checked out of the sneak.*
>
> *"I usually try to find the soft spot in a defense....There was no soft spot. So it was kind of a no-brainer to check to a toss play," Reynolds said of pitching the ball to Demond Brown, who sauntered in to cement a 45–20 victory.*
>
> *"What we called was a good play," said Niumatalolo, "but [Keenan] wanted the best play."*

Reynolds set the record the following week with four touchdowns in a 55–14 rout of SMU. He set the FBS record for touchdowns (eighty-eight), points (528) and yards rushing (4,559), the most in NCAA history. His senior year was the first and only time Navy won eleven games in 136 seasons.

After he was drafted by the Baltimore Ravens, Reynolds's number, 19, was retired by Navy, a historic nod for a player who arrived with almost no fanfare and became one of the most accomplished players in program history. "You come in slighted, feeling like people don't think you're good enough to be where you are, and that alone drive guys to achieve things that nobody expects out of them," Reynolds said. "This is what happens when you get guys playing together that have that chip on their shoulder."

# G.O.A.T.S.

## COACHES

## EDDIE EDRELATZ, 1950–58
## 50-26-8 (.642)

Eddie Erdelatz returned to Annapolis to catch and surpass one man, Army's Earl Blaik, and that's exactly what he did.

A former Navy assistant in 1945–47 and San Francisco 49ers coach for two years after that, Erdelatz replaced George Sauer, who took the head coach's job at Baylor. Erdelatz inherited a team short on the kind of depth needed to combat a brutally difficult schedule. He lost six of his first eight games before facing a monumental task in Earl Blaik's Black Knights to end 1950.

When asked about Army feeling slighted about being ranked No. 2 behind Oklahoma, Erdelatz invoked his sharp wit: "We're burned up, too. We're ranked 65th and should be 64th."[59] But the joke was on Army. Erdelatz inserted a unique offensive scheme, depending on blocking assignments, with ends split or set together and backs sometimes lined up as flankers. Navy's attack thrived, while the undefeated Cadets, twenty-one-point favorites, found themselves off-balance. The Midshipmen stunned Blaik's best team, 14–2.

The next year, while Erdelatz continued to build the foundation for some of Navy's best teams ever, ninety Cadets were separated—including thirty-seven football players[60]—in a massive honor code scandal at West Point.

Lackluster results (2-6-1) spoiled 1951, but Erdelatz racked up forty-five wins in sixty-six games over the next seven seasons. In 1954, the "Team Named Desire" went 8-2, beating Stanford (25–0) and Army (27–20) to earn the program's first bowl game since the 1924 Rose Bowl. Legendary Army coach Earl Blaik called these Midshipmen "the smartest, fastest Navy team I've ever seen."[61] A thirty-year drought quenched, Navy whitewashed Mississippi, 21–0, at the Sugar Bowl at Tulane Stadium.

In 1957, Navy went 9-1-1, beating Georgia (27–14) and Notre Dame (20–6) and shutting out Army, 14–0. That put Navy into the Cotton Bowl, and Erdelatz delivered a 20–7 win over Rice.

After a 6-3 mark in 1958, Erdelatz resigned from Navy unceremoniously. An ever-widening breach between the Academy and how Erdelatz executed the football program in accordance with Academy policies could not be repaired, and when his dalliance with the opening at Texas A&M became public, his days were numbered. He was fired in the spring of 1959 and replaced by Wayne Hardin. He returned to the Bay Area to coach the Oakland Raiders for the 1959 season.

Under Erdelatz, Navy recruited five First Team All-Americans: Steve Eisenhauer, Ronnie Beagle, Bob Reifsnyder, Joe Bellino and Greg Mather. Beagle, Reifsnyder and Bellino won the Maxwell Trophy. Bellino won the Heisman Trophy in 1960, too. Hardin, Erdelatz's successor, recruited another Maxwell and Heisman winner: Roger Staubach.

A side note to the Erdelatz era requires mention of Navy–Marine Corps Stadium. Municipal Stadium, site of Navy's biggest home games annually, was converted into what would become Memorial Stadium. Bill Veeck relocated his St. Louis Browns to Baltimore and rechristened them the Orioles in 1954, while the Baltimore Colts were cementing a relationship with the city that lasted until 1984. The Midshipmen were essentially squeezed out on Thirty-Third Street.

A long-term replacement for twelve-thousand-seat Thompson Stadium was patently necessary. Erdelatz's sustained success, including a 5-3-1 record against Blaik and wins in the Sugar and Colton Bowls, are primary reasons why Navy was able to successfully fundraise for and construct the original Academy stadium on Rowe Boulevard.

# WAYNE HARDIN 1959–64
## 38-22-2 (.629)

An assistant coach hired under Eddie Erdelatz, Wayne Hardin walked into the head coach's position at Navy like a chef walks into a pantry stocked with rib-sticking food—hungry and determined to carve up the competition.

The selection of Erdelatz's protégé was as contentious as the decision to fire Erdelatz. But Hardin not only kept the ship righted, he also pushed the program even higher in his six years. He won thirty-eight of sixty games—including a perfect record in six seasons at Navy-Marine Corps Stadium—and reached the Orange and Cotton Bowls, where Navy played Texas for the national title in 1963. Oh, yeah, he also recruited and coached Joe Bellino and Roger Staubach, Navy's only Heisman Trophy winners. "Eddie Erdelatz was a good man who did a great job," Hardin said. "The first thing I learned when Eddie hired me was to always answer the call."

So, after coaching his first game at Navy's new stadium, he received some feedback. "I got a letter from a lady, and I use that term tongue-in-cheek, who told me, 'I don't think you should be the head coach at Navy,'" Hardin said. "She went on to say, 'One of the things I can't stand is you don't wear a hat. Without a hat, I get blinded by the sun reflecting off your bald head!'"

Hardin replied and wore a hat from that point forward, and it ultimately became one of his trademarks, like the way Bill Belichick wears a hooded sweatshirt. "I never heard from her again," Hardin said.

Of course, it really didn't matter what he wore. His Navy teams were outstanding, until the Mids—who were returning Staubach as a senior—skidded to a 3-6-1 mark. It cost him his job. "I can't tell you why the 1964 season failed. It just wasn't good," Hardin said. "I have to take as much blame as the kids. We won together and we lost together, and that was how it ended."

Fired following that season, Hardin wouldn't resurface until 1970 at Temple. The Owls were a program floundering, but Hardin raised their profile, and in 1979, Temple went 9-2 and defeated California, 28–17, in the Garden State Bowl. He was 80-52-2 in thirteen seasons at Temple.

Bill Belichick, a winner of five Super Bowls, credited Hardin for showing him how innovation and risk-taking can pay big benefits. "I learned from him that there's nothing wrong with being aggressive," Belichick told *CSN New England* in January 2016. "He was very innovative in the kicking game....I still remember some of the things he did that were...they were brilliant. They were just brilliant."

Hardin had plenty of brilliant moments at Navy. He was the last coach to beat Notre Dame until a forty-three-game losing streak was broken by Paul Johnson in 2007. He won the first game with Air Force in 1960, and he won the most important of Army-Navy games: the 1963 battle played under the pall of the assassination of John F. Kennedy.

Hardin is also the only Navy coach to beat Notre Dame three times in four years—1960, 1961 and 1963. The Mids posted wins over the Fighting Irish in 2007, 2009 and 2010, split between Johnson and Niumatalolo.

When Navy hosted Temple in the 2016 American Athletic Conference title game, Hardin returned to Annapolis for the final time and conducted the coin toss. The last interview he conducted was for this book. Hardin passed on April 12, 2017.

With an overall record of 118-74-8 (.610), Hardin was inducted into the College Football Hall of Fame in 2013.

# GEORGE WELSH 1973–81
## 55-46-1 (.544)

The winningest coach at the University of Virginia and Atlantic Coast Conference history is also a Naval Academy legend. George Welsh, an outstanding quarterback for the Midshipmen during the school's "Camelot" era, resurrected Navy between 1973 and 1981. It was a welcome respite during a prolonged era of dismal results from the mid-1960s until Paul Johnson returned to Annapolis in 2002.

Welsh led the Mids to three bowl games and owned the battle for the Commander-in-Chief Trophy, winning the 170-pound prize five times, while retaining it twice and losing it just once. He went 6-3 against Air Force and 7-1-1 against Army, accomplishments that will be forgotten by no one in Annapolis, except maybe Welsh. "I thought I was really good against Army, but Johnson and Niumatalolo have accomplished something no one ever thought they'd see," Welsh said in a 2017 interview. "Fourteen straight against Army is a record you could never imagine."

A Navy quarterback in 1953–55 from Coaldale, Pennsylvania, Welsh led the Midshipmen over heavily favored Mississippi in the 1955 Sugar Bowl. He completed eight of fourteen passes for 76 yards while Navy ground out 442 total yards. As a senior, Welsh finished third in Heisman Trophy voting, leading the nation in passing and total offense.

Seven years of active duty and ten seasons under Joe Paterno at Penn State (1963–72) brought Welsh to Annapolis. But it almost didn't happen. "I was offered at Princeton, but they wanted to wait two or three weeks before hiring," Welsh said. "Navy knew I had the offer at Princeton, but I was the guy Navy wanted."

When Welsh took over, Navy had one winning season since 1964, and Penn State, Pitt, Notre Dame and Michigan were regulars on the schedule. By 1978, Welsh had Navy steaming. The Midshipmen opened 7-0, swept Air Force and Army and finished 9-3 by upsetting Jim McMahon and BYU, 23–16, in the first Holiday Bowl. His 1980 squad, which finished 8-4, played Houston in the Garden State Bowl. The players took their final exams the day before the game and were overwhelmed on the field, 35–0. "There was a culture clash within the administration of how important football should be at the academy," Welsh said. "There's no way you're going to be successful doing that."

In 1981, Welsh's final season, the Mids went 7-4-1. After a 3–3 tie against Army and a 31–28 loss to Ohio State in the Liberty Bowl, Welsh left Annapolis as the winningest coach in program history, a title he held until Niumatalolo surpassed him. "Wasn't too bad for a service academy, was it? We recruited better players, had good quarterbacking and wideouts and had really strong offensive lines," Welsh said. "I wanted to see if I could compete consistently at the highest level of college football. The situation at Virginia was something I couldn't pass up."

Welsh was inducted into the College Football Hall of Fame in 2004.

## PAUL JOHNSON 2002–7
## 45-29 (.608)

Navy Athletic Director Chet Gladchuk had been on the job less than three weeks when he fired Head Coach Charlie Weatherbie, and forty-two days later, he handed Paul Johnson the helm on December 9, 2001.

The *Baltimore Sun* described the program in a headline as a "winless ship" above a story announcing his hire. "Rudderless" would have been a better description. Navy had lost twenty of the last twenty-one and thirty-two of forty-one. Johnson, Weatherbie's offensive coordinator in 1995–96, left Navy for Georgia Southern and won two FCS national titles en route to a 62-10 record, while Weatherbie went 16-39 in the same five-year period after signing a ten-year, $6 million contract.

Johnson had earned the lion's share of the credit for Navy's resurgence in the mid-1990s, but his first season as head coach was disastrous. After opening with a 38–7 win over hapless Southern Methodist, Navy lost the next ten games, surrendering 417 points. More than half of those losses were beheadings. But in the final game of the season in Giants Stadium, Navy pounded rival Army, 58–12, giving just enough hope that Johnson's option plan could thrive.

The next season, and the four years to follow, Johnson and his Midshipmen rolled over opponents, winning forty-three of the next sixty-two games from 2003 to 2007. While most major college football programs were moving into throw-first, spread offenses designed to exploit speed and size and, later, RPOs (run-pass options), Navy's scheme of cut blocking fueled a 10-2 mark in 2004, the first ten-win season for the program in ninety-nine years.

Johnson bristled at the presumption that Navy—and the two other service academies—can only win with the triple option. "Offense is offense and you do what you do," Johnson said in a 2004 interview with the *Baltimore Sun*.[62] "A lot of different schools run the option and I don't think you can say that you can only do certain things at certain places. I don't know why people say that."

Johnson took the Mids to five straight bowls but, more importantly, went 11-1 against Army and Air Force, earning the Commander-in-Chief Trophy—which they hadn't won since 1981—five consecutive seasons and defeating Army in all six meetings.

In Johnson's final season, Navy was 8-4, including a 46–44 win in triple overtime over Notre Dame, snapping an NCAA-record forty-three-game losing streak to the Irish that dated back to 1963. Air Force didn't debut on the Navy schedule until 1960 and wasn't an annual game until 1972. By defeating Notre Dame, Air Force and Army, 2007 was the first season the Midshipmen defeated their three primary rivals in forty-seven years.

Citing an opportunity for a new challenge—specifically to win a national championship—Johnson accepted the Georgia Tech job on December 7, following the November 26 firing of Chan Gailey, a week after trouncing Army, 38–3, in Baltimore.

Junior fullback Eric Kettani, who would go on to play four seasons in the NFL, told the *Washington Post*, "He beat Army and Air Force and Notre Dame. What else can you do? He told us his goal is to win a national championship. You can't blame him for that."[63]

Johnson rebuilt the Navy program into a perennial bowl program in just six years and drew a sustainable blueprint for his successor to follow. "If I had any doubt in the system and what we were trying to do, I affirmed it at the Academy," Johnson said in reflecting on his time at Navy in 2017. "I learned you don't have to have the best players to win. If guys will buy in, work hard and play together, you can be successful."

## KEN NIUMATALOLO 2008–PRESENT
## 77-42 (.643)

When his two boys, Va'a and Ali'i, played football at Annapolis's Broadneck High School, Ken Niumatalolo would sometimes watch from the tennis courts situated high above the corner of the field's end zone, far removed from the few thousand parents, students and fans populating the Bruins' home games. Staying out of the fray is a far cry from his early days at Navy. It's hard to believe, but the winningest coach in Navy history was fired by the Academy at the McDonald's on Ritchie Highway in Arnold, Maryland.

Charlie Weatherbie was the Navy head coach who delivered the ambush. Niumatalolo, then twenty-nine, has always taken the high road. "I was a young, hot-head coach who thought he had all the answers," Niumatalolo said. "I have to own some of that situation."

The journey that got Niumatalolo fired was also his pathway to becoming the winningest coach in school history. It is a story unlike any in college football, at any level. He had ascended to the offensive coordinator's position after Paul Johnson left Navy for the head coach's position at Georgia Southern. The Midshipmen went 7-4 in 1997 but stumbled to a 3-8 finish in 1998.

During those two years, when Charlie Weatherbie had suggestions, Niumatalolo brazenly challenged his boss, saying things like, "Why are we doing that? That's stupid!" Ultimately, it cost him his job but also laid the groundwork for him to become an outstanding head coach. "I think Kenny learned a great deal under Charlie," Johnson said. "Kenny's such a good guy. No one would think he's got that kind of temper. But I think that taught him how to manage situations better—and not just the temper."

After Weatherbie fired him, Niumatalolo landed on his feet with a coaching position at UNLV under John Robinson. "I went from being a pretty vocal, outspoken assistant—I challenged everything and had a strong opinion on how to do things—to being fired and sitting in the back of staff meetings at UNLV and taking notes," Niumatalolo said.

He returned to Navy in 2002 as an assistant to Johnson. He became head coach for the 2007 Poinsettia Bowl when Johnson left for Georgia Tech. Now entering his tenth season, Niumatalolo owns eight wins over Army, five over Air Force and three over Notre Dame, while leading Navy to nine straight bowl games and seventy-seven wins.

Since 2003, when Niumatalolo was first an offensive line coach and later assistant head coach and ultimately head coach, Navy has compiled an astounding 120-61 (.663) record. The staff he's largely kept intact is responsible for fourteen straight wins over Army, winning seven consecutive Commander-in-Chief Trophies and earning an NCAA-record four rushing titles in a row.

In a cutthroat industry where many coaches are hired to be fired, Niumatalolo has become a lighthouse at the end of Navy's football pier. "Of all the things that I'm most proud of here, not only are we winning, but we're winning the right way," Niumatalolo said. "I'm just as competitive as I was on Day 1, and the rings from the bowl games are great and dandy, but the proudest thing is the guys graduate from here."

# POTPOURRI

## REMEMBERING ALTON GRIZZARD

The worst kind of tale, of unfulfilled promise and unfathomable tragedy, stunned the Navy football program in 1993. Alton Grizzard, a popular Navy quarterback from 1987 to 1990, and Kerryn O'Neill, an Academy track star, were murdered on December 1, 1993, at the hands of an unhinged USNA classmate at the Naval Amphibious Base in Coronado, California.

As detailed in her obituary in the *New York Times*, O'Neill, an ensign, had once pledged to marry George Smith, her former Academy classmate who was also an ensign. But the two had quarreled heavily, and she had decided to end the relationship. Smith was beside himself, and he had penned O'Neill a thirteen-page letter, but the obsessive overture only solidified her decision. Knowing he was scheduled to shove off for tour on a submarine within the next twenty-four hours, Smith knocked on O'Neill's door at around 1:45 a.m. that Wednesday morning, armed with lover's lament and a loaded .9-millimeter, semiautomatic Ruger.

When Grizzard opened the door, Smith snapped and shot his former classmate dead with four shots. Smith then went after O'Neill, and he killed his former fiancée with a shot to the head while she hid behind a chair. He then turned the gun on himself and died in an ambulance on the way to a hospital.

*Left*: Kerryn O'Neill. *Right*: Alton Grizzard. *USNA Sports Information*/The Trident.

Friends of all three victims from Annapolis to Coronado and Navy ports stretching across the deep blue sea all said that O'Neill and Grizzard were not romantically involved.

News of the murders stunned the Academy. "They brought us into the football building and told us, and it was stunned silence, and later rage," said Navy linebacker Clint Bruce, then a plebe. "When you're at an academy, you know you're preparing for war, but to lose a brother, the way we did, is a moment I'll never forget."

The tragedy juxtaposed that week's usually celebratory Army-Navy game and made national headlines. Coach George Chaump broke down when the news was broken to the team, and quarterback Jim Kubiak described it as a "nightmare."[64]

Four days after Grizzard's death, the Mids met Army in Giants Stadium, wearing stickers on their helmets that read "GRIZ." After spotting the Cadets a sixteen-point lead, Navy roared back within 16–14 and had the ball on Army's one when Ryan Bucchianeri came in to kick the game-winning field goal. With rain pelting down, his kick passed the wrong side of the right upright with six seconds left. With the kick missed, Bucchianeri stared lifelessly into space while the Cadets stormed off the field jubilantly. For the second time in four days, Navy was left stunned and heartbroken.

*"I've kicked that ball right through the uprights 1,000 times in my head,"*
*said Bucchianeri, a native of Monongahela, the western Pennsylvania*
*town that produced quarterback Joe Montana. "I'll go to sleep tonight*
*believing I did my best. It all happened so fast, I can't say what went*
*wrong. I just missed it."*[65]

In the weeks following the game, stories of the funerals and the investigation dominated the news cycle. From O'Neill's obit in the *Times*: "Navy officers have sent their condolences from ships in the Pacific and bases across the country. An admiral called from Guam."

In an article recalling Grizzard from the *Baltimore Sun*: "They came from throughout the country. There were Navy SEALS from the U.S. Naval Amphibious Base in Coronado, Cal., where Lt. Grizzard was stationed. Classmates serving as officers in the fleet returned to the academy from Navy ports."

There's a wound in the hearts of Grizzard's teammates likely never to close, and the lingering bewilderment of why—why did this have to happen? In the same *Times* article, Grizzard's high school football coach, Thomas Rhoades, said, "I thought [Alton] was the kind of kid the whole country would read about one day, but not like this."

Grizzard prepped in Virginia Beach, Virginia, and racked up 5,666 career all-purpose yards, becoming the Academy's all-time leader in that department. O'Neill, an ocean engineer, set three track and field records as a Midshipman. She was buried in Wilkes-Barre, Pennsylvania; he was interred at Arlington Cemetery.

Military training prepares Midshipmen in Annapolis and Cadets at West Point and Colorado Springs, Colorado, for the sudden loss of a sailor, soldier or airman, but what prepares anyone for the horror that played out in the darkness of that Coronado, California morning?

Lives well lived inexplicably cut short. No fulfillment of a career. No goodbye.

## THE TRIPLE-OPTION OFFENSE

Since December 7, 2002, when the Midshipmen overwhelmed Army, 58–12, the Midshipmen are 120–61, a .663 winning percentage. It's a staggering record of success after nearly forty years of futility.

What changed everything for Navy was one man and his offense: Paul Johnson and the triple-option. The option strips your instinct away because you're unsure who will have the ball or what they'll do with it. When you're tip-toeing on just about every play, you're done. "The offense works and it's timeless," Niumatalolo said. "It's not a gimmick offense. It's based on numbers, sound principles and sound concepts."

Today, the acronym you hear most about college football offenses is RPO (run-pass option), and it's based on the same formula that governs the triple-option decision-making. "If you're here, throw the ball over there. If you're on this side, throw to that side. If you read zone-weak, you go here with the ball," Niumatalolo said. "This scheme, offensively, gave us a chance to compete at the next level."

That's the key covenant of the triple offense because Navy can't line up and run a conventional offense. George Chaump, who ran a traditional pro-set offense from 1990 to 1994, won just fourteen games and lost about a half-dozen quarterbacks to injuries. Physically, opponents were too big, and because of the military obligations and size requirements, Navy couldn't recruit enough players able to protect skill-positioned players to be successful in that offense.

Niumatalolo credits offensive coordinator Ivin Jasper with keeping the core foundation of the offense in place while evolving the attack to counter natural adjustments opponents make to defeat it. "What we do is definitely a benefit in today's world with spread passing and throwing the ball all over the place," Niumatalolo said. "Most schools only see this one time a year in our conference. The current questions that we're facing, and finding answers for them, is solving the struggle moving the ball against the other service academies."

There's only four plays to defend: the fullback dive, the quarterback keep, the pitch to the slotback and a pass. Opposing coaches despise it and tried to outlaw it. Johnson, who was on the NCAA rules committee during a portion of his time at Navy, was like a public defender taking on a mob lining up against the option offense. "If something gets a reputation, it becomes fact without any statistical evidence to back it up," Johnson said. "You get people talking about getting hurt, saying it's dangerous and without any statistics to support it. That's the thing that drove me crazy."

In *Bad Boys*, the 2013 ESPN 30 for 30 documentary, former Detroit Piston and Hall of Fame guard Joe Dumars talked about how the Pistons would travel from city to city in the late 1980s and early 1990s, reading articles in the local paper about how their opponent was ready to stand up and fight the Pistons. That kind of mental edge was something Johnson's offense invited. "As long as [opposing] coaches got it in their head that we cut block on the perimeter way more than the other team, that was OK," Johnson said. "I didn't have a problem with it."

But whatever the scheme, if you're successful with it, the coaching industry will come after it. When rival coaches talked about outlawing his bread and butter, Johnson did the same. "I'd go to the annual coaches meeting, and someone who threw the ball would say something like, 'We need to outlaw blocking below the waist,' I would say, 'OK. That's cool. Let's outlaw tackling below the waist. Let's do away with all blocking below the waist, not just on the perimeter, so your backs can't pick up blitzes,'" Johnson said. "Then you'd hear something like, 'That's not what we're talking about…' What we were talking about is [they] don't like to play against it. It doesn't have anything to do with injuries. I did feel like anyone who ran the option had to defend themselves and their program."

# NOTES

## Chapter 1

1. Jack Clary, *Erdelatz and the Fabulous Fifties: Navy Football, Gridiron Legends and Fighting Heroes* (Annapolis, MD: Naval Institute Press, 1997), 110–11.
2. Ibid.
3. Ibid., 121.
4. Ibid., 127.
5. Joseph M. Sheehan, "Navy's Pass Nips Michigan, 20–14," *New York Times*, October 12, 1958, retrieved from http://www.timesmachine.nytimes.com.
6. Clary, *Erdelatz and the Fabulous Fifties*, 134.
7. Ibid., 135.
8. Gary Lambrecht, "50 Years Later the 1963 Navy Football Team Still Ranks as the Best in School History," Navy Sports, October 2, 2013, http://www.navysports.com/sports/m-footbl/spec-rel/100213aaa.html.
9. Ibid.

## Chapter 2

10. Clary, *Erdelatz and the Fabulous Fifties*, 167.
11. Anthony Cotton, "Naval Academy Dismisses Football Coach Uzelac," *Washington Post*, December 12, 1989, retrieved from http://www.washingtonpost.com.

12. Alan Goldstein, "Chaump Shipped Out as Navy Coach," *Baltimore Sun*, December 5, 1994, retrieved from http://www.baltimoresun.com.

## Chapter 3

13. Mark Schlabach, "Navy Gives Air Force the Boot," *Washington Post*, October 1, 2004, retrieved from www.washingtonpost.com.
14. Kent Baker, "Navy Finishes Off Air Force," *Baltimore Sun*, October 9, 2005, retrieved from www.baltimoresun.com.
15. Camille Powell, "Navy Makes It Six in a Row vs. Air Force," *Washington Post*, October 5, 2008, retrieved from www.washingtonpost.com.
16. T.C. Cameron, "Official Doesn't Deserve Blame," Baltimore Sun Media Group, October 18, 2011, retrieved from http://www.hometownannapolis.com.
17. Don Markus, "Former Navy Football Players Sorting Out Their Future After Breaking Regulations," Baltimore Sun Media Group, August 20, 2012, retrieved from http://www.baltimoresun.com.
18. T.C. Cameron, "Mission Nearly Accomplished for Navy's 'Big Play C.J.,'" Baltimore Sun Media Group, December 11, 2014, retrieved from www.capitalgazette.com.

## Chapter 5

19. *Pearl Harbor*, Michael Bay, director, Touchstone, 2001.
20. *Mutual Respect: Onward Notre Dame*, NBC Sports, October 8, 2015.
21. Henry C. Herge, *Inception of Navy College Training Programs*, Navy V-12, 1996, page 20.
22. *Mutual Respect.*
23. Lou Somogyi, "Notre-Dame-Navy: Numbers, Turning Point & More," *Blue&Gold*, November 5, 2016, retrieved from http://www.notredame.rivals.com.
24. *Mutual Respect.*
25. Ibid.
26. Ibid.
27. Ibid.
28. *Chicago Tribune*, "Irish Rally in 4th to Beat Navy 14–6," November 3, 1974, retrieved from http://www.archives.chicagotribune.com.

29. Michael Janofsky, "Notre Dame Kick Beats Navy," *New York Times*, November 4, 1984, retrieved from http://www.newyorktimes.com.

30. Ibid.

31. *Mutual Respect.*

32. Alan Goldstein, "Navy Ends 2 Yards Short of Notre Dame," *Baltimore Sun*, November 2, 1997, retrieved from http://www.baltimoresun.com.

33. Kent Baker, "Irish Inch Past Navy," *Baltimore Sun*, October 31, 1999, retrieved from http://www.baltimoresun.com.

34. *Mutual Respect.*

35. Ibid.

36. Ibid.

## Chapter 6

37. Christian Swezey, "Their Ship Comes In," *Washington Post*, November 4, 2007, retrieved from www.washingtonpost.com.

## Chapter 7

38. John Feinstein, "Trent Steelman Lives Up to the Best of the Army-Navy Game, Even in Defeat," *Washington Post*, December 8, 2012, retrieved from www.washingtonpost.com.

## Chapter 8

39. Dan Wetzel, Josh Peter and Jeff Passan, "The Cartel," *Death to the BCS: The Definitive Case Against the Bowl Championship Series* (New York: Gotham, 2010), 3.

40. Ibid., "Lies, Damn Lies, and Bowl Payouts," *Death to the BCS*, 35.

41. Doug Lesmerises, "Could the Navy Game Have Played a Role in Ohio State's Loss to Virginia Tech?," Cleveland.com, September 14, 2014, retrieved from http://www.cleveland.com.

## *Appendix I*

42. Richard Weintraub, "Game in the Shadows," ESPN, 2009, retrieved from http://www.espn.com/espn/eticket/story.

43. Ibid.

44. Ibid.

45. Clary, *Erdelatz and the Fabulous Fifties*, 243.

46. Ibid., 235.

47. Ibid., 237.

48. Herman Hickman, "Navy 21, Mississippi 0," *Sports Illustrated*, www.SI.com/vault.

49. Morris A. Bealle, *Gangway for Navy*, 1st ed. (Washington, D.C.: Columbia Pub., 1951), 140.

## *Appendix II*

50. National Football Foundation, "Frank 'Wick' Wickhorst," http://www.footballfoundation.org/Programs/CollegeFootballHallofFame/SearchDetail.aspx?id=20025.

## *Appendix III*

51. Clary, *Erdelatz and the Fabulous Fifties*, 118.

52. Alan Goldstein, "Hall Enlists Another Mid," *Baltimore Sun*, December 9, 1997, retrieved from http://www.articles.baltimoresun.com.

53. Ibid.

54. Ibid.

55. Barry Wilner and Ken Rappoport, "Navy's Heisman Heroes," *Gridiron Glory: The Story of the Army-Navy Football Rivalry* (Lanham, MD: Taylor Trade, 2005), 91.

56. Ibid.

57. Mike Klingaman, "Catching Up with…Former Navy Running Back Eddie Meyers," *Baltimore Sun*, October 22, 2015, retrieved from http://www.baltimoresun.com.

58. Ibid., November 19, 2015, retrieved from http://www.baltimoresun.com.

## Appendix IV

59. Jack Clary, *Army vs. Navy: 70 Years of Football Rivalry* (New York: Ronald Press Company, 1965), 205.

60. Ibid., 212.

61. Ibid., 234

62. *Baltimore Sun*, "Staff Report: Q&A with Navy Football Coach Paul Johnson," January 12, 2004, retrieved from www.baltimoresun.com.

63. Christian Swezey, "Johnson Leaves Navy for Georgia Tech," *Washington Post*, December 8, 2007, retrieved from www.washingtonpost.com.

## Appendix V

64. Wilner and Rappoport, "Rekindling the Rivalry," *Gridiron Glory*, 120.

65. Alan Goldstein, "Navy Comeback Gets the Boot: It's Army, 16–14," *Baltimore Sun*, December 5, 1993, retrieved from http://www.baltimoresun.com.

# ABOUT THE AUTHOR

Author and journalist T.C. Cameron covered sports and the Naval Academy for the *Capital-Gazette* newspapers, part of the Baltimore Sun Media Group, from 2009 to 2015. This is his third title with Arcadia Publishing and The History Press, having published *Metro Detroit's High School Football Rivalries* (2008) and *Metro Detroit's High School Basketball Rivalries* (2009). Cameron holds a degree in communications from Eastern Michigan University and has been an Annapolis resident since 2009. He's an unabashed fan of the narrative found in sports.

*Visit us at*
www.historypress.net
..............................................................
*This title is also available as an e-book*